Biblical baby names *for Today*

Meera Lester

adamsmedia
avon, massachusetts

Published by
Adams Media, an F+W Publications Company
57 Littlefield Street, Avon, MA 02322. U.S.A.
www.adamsmedia.com

ISBN-10: 1-59869-553-3
ISBN-13: 978-1-59869-553-3

Printed in Canada

J I H G F E D C B A

Library of Congress Cataloging-in-Publication Data
is available from the publisher.

This publication is designed to provide accurate and authori-
tative information with regard to the subject matter covered.
It is sold with the understanding that the publisher is not
engaged in rendering legal, accounting, or other professional
advice. If legal advice or other expert assistance is required,
the services of a competent professional person should be
sought.

> —From a *Declaration of Principles* jointly adopted by a
> Committee of the American Bar Association and
> a Committee of Publishers and Associations

Many of the designations used by manufacturers and sell-
ers to distinguish their product are claimed as trademarks.
Where those designations appear in this book and Adams
Media was aware of a trademark claim, the designations
have been printed with initial capital letters.

Contains material adopted and abridged from *The Everything®
Bible Stories Book* by Michael Paydos, Copyright © 2002 by
F+W Publications, Inc., and *The Everything® Baby Names Book,
2nd Edition* by June Rifkin, Copyright © 2006 by F+W Publications, Inc.

*This book is available at quantity discounts for bulk purchases.
For information, please call 1-800-289-0963.*

Contents

Introduction

Choosing a name for your baby is one of the most important tasks you will undertake during your pregnancy because your child will have that name for the rest of his or her life. While some parents desire a name that reflects the family's ethnic lineage, spiritual roots, or cultural heritage, others hope the name they choose will convey a sense of individuality or destiny. Some expectant couples even believe that a name sets up a vibration or energy field around the child that serves him or her throughout life. Your child's name to some degree imparts an aspect of his or her persona to the world and may even affect interactions with others.

Whether you are drawn to old biblical names, names of historical religious figures such as Jesus' disciples or Christian saints, names that have evolved from certain Latin words (such as those meaning honor, justice, prosperity, truth, glory, and so on), or simply names that in some way reflect the ancient world, you will find many names to choose from in this book.

Not only are over 1,000 names listed, but each entry includes the name's origin and meaning, if it is known, as well as biblical, mythological, religious, or historic figures who had that name. Most names also list biblical citations so that you can easily locate the name in the text of the Bible. In certain instances when a name is associated with biblical narrative, an anecdote or retelling of that narrative is given.

If you already know the gender of your baby, you can narrow your search to the names of either boy or girl. While Mary remains perhaps the most popular biblical female name of all time, Hannah, Eve, Rachel, and Abigail increasingly are being chosen as notable women of the Old Testament and for their relevance in biblical history. Perhaps the most popular biblical name for a boy is Jacob. But numerous others such as Joseph, Moses, Benjamin, Adam, and Joshua are gaining ground, sometimes with unusual spellings. Biblical names from Hebrew, Arabic, Latin, Greek, and other origins have unique appeal because the name often can be traced back through centuries of use and many are preserved in Judeo-Christian tradition's ancient and holiest book—the Bible.

Have fun reading this book, perusing the names, and discovering some of the fascinating stories found in the Bible that often illustrate some of the larger-than-life characters whose names are sprinkled throughout the Old and New Testaments.

Part One
boy
names

A

AARON *(Hebrew)* Exalted; enlightened. NOTABLES: Biblical brother of Moses and Miriam (Exodus 4:14). VARIATIONS: Aahron, Aaran, Aaraon, Aaren, Aarin, Aeron, Aharon, Ahran, Ahren, Aran, Arek, Aren, Aron, Aronek, Aronne, Aronos, Arran, Arren, Arrin, Arron.

Aaron Anointed as the Jews' First High Priest

Aaron belonged to the ancient Hebrew tribe of Levi. He was the son of Jochebed and Amram. Aaron's younger brother, Moses, was chosen by God to lead the Hebrews away from their Egyptian enslavement to freedom in Canaan. Aaron served as a diplomatic and articulate spokesperson for Moses to Pharaoh and the Hebrew people. God didn't just empower Moses to show miraculous signs; he also blessed Aaron with that gift. At the behest of the Lord, Aaron cast down his rod before Pharaoh, and it became a serpent. Pharaoh, in turn, called upon his sorcerers and wise men to show their own signs. The Bible says that certain men serving Pharaoh "did in like manner with their enchantments. For they cast down every man his rod, and they became serpents: but Aaron's rod swallowed up their rods" (Exodus 7:11–12).

After the Jews left Egypt and God gave Moses the Torah, or the laws of the Jewish people, Aaron became the first High Priest of Israel. He was anointed, given priestly robes, and instructed in his duties. He and his older sister Miriam continued to accompany the Jews and their leader Moses to the Promised Land. But during Moses's extended absence on the way to Canaan, Aaron yielded to the demands of the people to produce an idol. He created a golden calf as an image of the divine that they could worship. His intention was to appease them and to prevent further dissension until Moses could return. But God punished Aaron by not permitting him to enter the Promised Land. He died in the desert just before the people crossed over into Canaan.

ABADDON *(Hebrew)* Knows God. NOTABLES: A beast from the abyss destined to become the angelic king Abaddon mentioned in the Book of Revelation (Revelation 9:11).

ABBA *(Hebrew)* Father. NOTABLES: Jesus' name for God the Father (Mark 14:36). VARIATIONS: Abbas.

ABBEY *(Hebrew)* A form of Abe or Abraham. VARIATIONS: Abbe, Abbie, Abby.

ABBOTT *(Hebrew)* Father. VARIATIONS: Abbitt, Abbot, Abott.

ABEDNEGO *(Hebrew)* Servant or worshipper of Nebo. NOTABLES: A Hebrew who refused to worship the golden image that Babylonian King Nebuchadnezzar had established (Daniel 3:14–18).

ABEL *(Hebrew)* Breathing spirit or breath. NOTABLES: Biblical son of Adam and Eve who was the keeper of the sheep (Genesis 4:2). VARIATIONS: Abell, Able, Avel.

ABIAH *(Hebrew)* Child of God. VARIATIONS: Abia, Aviya.

ABIATHAR *(Hebrew)* Father of abundance; of plenty. NOTABLES: Biblical son of Ahimelech who showed David that King Saul had slain priests of the Lord (1 Samuel 22:20–21).

ABIHU *(Hebrew)* God is mine. NOTABLES: Biblical son of Aaron and Elisheba, daughter of Amminadab (Exodus 6:23).

ABIJAH *(Hebrew)* Possessor or worshipper of Yahweh. NOTABLES: The second son of Samuel; son of King Jeroboam I (1 Kings 14: 1).

ABNER *(Hebrew)* Father of light. NOTABLES: The captain of the host for King Saul (1 Samuel 17:55). VARIATIONS: Ab, Aviner, Avner.

ABRAHAM *(Hebrew)* Father of many. NOTABLES: Biblical patriarch Abraham. VARIATIONS: Abe, Abrahamo, Abrahan, Abram, Abramo, Abran, Abrao, Avraham, Avram, Avrum, Ibrahim.

ABRAM *(Hebrew)* Form of Abraham. NOTABLES: Original name of Abraham the patriarch. VARIATIONS: Abrams, Avram, Avrom.

Abraham Deceives Pharaoh

After God caused a great flood to cover the earth, the water that had washed iniquity from the world finally subsided. Great masses of land could again be lived upon. Noah and his family and all the plant and animal species that had escaped the deluge left the ark and began their lives anew.

Noah's sons Shem, Ham, and Japheth and their respective wives had families. Noah's descendants prospered and increased in number. Abram was one who prospered; he and his wife Sarai had no children, but he cared for his nephew Lot. God told Abram to leave for a new land. God would guide Abram.

Abram set off for Canaan with his family and friends, living as nomads as they traveled to Canaan. God came to Abram while he rested at the end of the long and arduous journey and told him, "Unto thy seed will I give this land: and there builded he an altar unto the Lord . . . "(Genesis 12:7).

A famine scourged the land, so Abram and his group continued onward toward Egypt. But before entering Pharaoh's land, Abram told Sarai that the Egyptians would see her beauty and kill him so they could give her to Pharaoh. Abram asked Sarai to tell them that she was his sister.

Just as Abram feared, Sarai was noticed by Pharaoh's men, who carried word back to the ruler about her beauty. Pharaoh sent for Abram and Sarai. He lavished gifts on Abram but took Sarai for his wife because he believed that Sarai was Abram's sister. The Lord sent plagues upon Pharaoh and his people because of his taking of Sarai. Sometime later when Pharaoh became ill, he asked Abram who he was that he had brought illness upon Egypt's ruler and why hadn't he told the truth about Sarai being his wife. Abram confessed the truth to Pharaoh.

Enraged, Pharaoh ordered Abram to take his wife and leave. Abram left Egypt and returned to the land where he had made an altar to the Lord. He and his group settled there with their animals. Abram and his nephew prospered.

Because the land could not accommodate the needs of their growing herds of cattle and sheep, people in Abram's and Lot's camps began bickering over the grazing rights. Abram told Lot that they should not be fighting—they belonged to the same family. Abram suggested that Lot could choose an area of land in which to settle and he, Abram, would find a place in the opposite direction. So Lot gazed at the plains of Jordan and the land that extended north that was nourished by numerous streams and was covered with trees and grass. Lot, his family, and his servants headed in that direction.

After Lot was gone, the Lord spoke to Abram. He told Abram, "Lift up now thine eyes, and look from the place where thou art northward, and southward, and eastward, and westward: for all the land which thou seest, to thee will I give it, and to thy seed forever." (Genesis 13:14–15) That place was the Plain of Mamre, which was also known as Hebron. It was there that Abram and his family moved their tent and settled. God had promised to make Abram's family grow and multiply through many generations. The land was God's gift to Abram because Abram had been generous to Lot.

ABSALOM *(Hebrew)* Father of peace. VARIATIONS: Absalaam, Absalon.

ACHISH *(Hebrew)* Angry. NOTABLES: Biblical king of Gath (1 Samuel 21:10).

ADAIAH *(Hebrew)* Witness of God. VARIATIONS: Adaia, Adaya.

ADAM *(Hebrew)* Man of the red earth. NOTABLES: First human that God created, who became the ancestral father of all humans (Genesis 1:27, 2:7). VARIATIONS: Adamec, Adamek, Adamh, Adamik, Adamka, Adamko, Adamo, Adams, Adamson, Adamsson, Adan, Adao, Addam, Addams, Addamson, Addie, Addis, Addy, Adhamh, Adnet, Adnot.

Adam and Eve and the First Sin

Adam means "the man" in Hebrew. He was the first human that God created. "And the Lord God formed man of the dust of the ground, and breathed into his nostrils the breath of life; and man became a living soul." (Genesis 2:7) God placed Adam, his favorite creation, in the Garden of Eden and charged Adam with caring for the garden. He told Adam that he could eat fruit from any of the trees in the garden, except for the Tree of Knowledge. Eating from that tree would bring death.

God determined that Adam should not be alone. He rounded up all the animals and brought them to Adam to name. No animal was a good match as a mate for Adam, so God decided to create the perfect companion. He caused Adam to fall into a deep sleep. After removing one of Adam's ribs, God formed another human—the first woman.

Adam named his companion Eve because she was to become the mother of all humankind. "Eve" means "the giver of life" in Hebrew.

Adam and Eve dwelled as husband and wife in the Garden of Eden. They cared for the land, tended the trees, and nourished themselves from the great variety of food available. Although they delighted in tasting the produce of many trees, they did not sample the fruit from the Tree of Knowledge that grew in the center of the garden. God had forbidden them to eat from that tree, and the couple obeyed their Creator . . . at first.

Sharing the garden with Adam and Eve was a serpent. Of all the animals that God had created, the serpent was the most clever and devious. He envied the humans because they were God's favorite among all his creations. One day, the serpent inquired of Eve whether or not God had actually forbidden them to partake of any fruit in the garden.

Eve clarified what God had told them. The only tree that they were forbidden to eat from was the one in the center of the garden. To eat from that tree could be perilous for them.

The serpent seemed to have some degree of superior knowledge, for it explained to the woman that she would not die and that instead she would gain knowledge of the difference between good and evil and that knowledge would make her like God.

With the serpent goading her on, Eve plucked the fruit from the forbidden tree and bit into it and then offered it to Adam. As the two munched away on the fruit, their minds became acutely aware of themselves and their surroundings. They realized that they were both naked. They forgot about eating and plucked some leaves to make coverings for themselves.

In the cool of the day, God drew near. Adam and Eve hid so their creator wouldn't see them. Although God knew where they were, he called out, "Adam, where are you?" An embarrassed Adam finally found the courage to speak. He told God that he had heard the Lord calling out to him but had crouched in the bushes because he was naked.

"How did you know you were naked? Did you eat the forbidden fruit from the Tree of Knowledge?" God wanted to know. Adam answered, yes, and explained how Eve had given him the fruit.

God turned to Eve and asked her if what Adam said was true.

Eve replied, "Yes."

God surely felt displeasure and disappointment. He had given his beloved humans the most beautiful place on earth to live. The only rule he had asked them to obey was to not eat from that tree. Not only would they have some difficult knowledge to grapple with, they also had the consequence of eventual death.

God cursed the serpent so that it would have to crawl on its belly to move around. Then he turned to Adam and Eve. He told them that from that moment on, they and all who come after them would toil to survive. They would have to grow their own food on land that would produce mostly weeds. They would one day die and return to dust.

What the serpent said to Eve wasn't a complete lie. After Adam and Eve ate the fruit from the Tree of Knowledge, they did gain the ability to understand the difference between good and evil. Each had a conscience and fully developed emotional sense. They could sense their own mortality.

God banished Adam and Eve from the Garden of Eden. No human being would ever be allowed to enter it again. To make sure nobody ever got near the Tree of Life again, God left an angel with a giant flaming sword to guard the garden's gateway (Genesis 3:24, Genesis 2, Genesis 3).

ADIV *(Hebrew)* Gentle.

ADLAI *(Hebrew)* My witness. VARIATIONS: Adalia, Adlay, Adley.

ADMON *(Hebrew)* Red peony.

ADONIJAH *(Hebrew)* Jehovah is my lord. NOTABLES: Biblical son of Haggith and King David (2 Samuel 3:4). VARIATIONS: Adon, Adonia, Adonijah, Adoniya, Adoniyah.

ADRIEL *(Hebrew)* God's flock. VARIATIONS: Adrial.

AENEAS *(Greek)* One who is praised. VARIATIONS: Aineas, Aineis, Eneas, Enneas.

AHAB *(Hebrew)* Father's brother. NOTABLES: King of Israel, the seventh such monarch. His father, whom he succeeded, was Omri.

Ahab—Politically Powerful but Spiritually Weak

Ahab, son of Omri, reigned for twenty-two years after he ascended to the throne as King of Israel. He married Jezebel, daughter of the King of Tyre, and thereby strengthened his kingdom's relationship with Tyre. New and improved trade between Tyre and the kingdom of

Israel meant greater wealth and an increased number of merchants among the Israelites. But the alliance had a negative impact. Jezebel and her people avidly worshipped Baal, a pagan god. Some accounts assert that she greatly influenced Ahab to introduce Baalism to the Israelites. Soon, curious Israelites began to become involved in the cult of Baal.

The Hebrew prophet Elijah the Tishbite became the voice of reason and Hebrew conscience. He challenged Ahab and Jezebel to be faithful to the God of Abraham and reject the pagan gods. Though biblical history records Ahab as a politically strong king who fortified certain cities and did a lot of building during his reign, he was also spiritually weak and unduly influenced by Jezebel and her almost fanatical commitment to Baalism. In a high moment of drama, the prophet Elijah confronted Ahab over the royal couple's theft of a vineyard (see "The Taking of Naboth's Vineyard" under NABOTH) and foretold the king's death.

Ahab engaged the Syrians to win back Ramoth in Gilead. In the fury of battle, a random arrow pierced Ahab's chest. "And a certain man drew a bow at a venture, and smote the king of Israel between the joints of the harness: wherefore he said unto the driver of his chariot, "Turn thine hand, and carry me out of the host; for I am wounded." And the battle increased that day: and the king was stayed up in his chariot against the Syrians, and died at evening: and the blood ran out of the wound into the midst of the chariot." (1 Kings 22:34–35) He died as a result of his injury, thus fulfilling Elijah's prophecy (1 Kings 22:37).

AHASUERUS *(Persian)* Mighty. NOTABLES: Considered by some to be identical with King Xerxes of Persia.

AHAZIAH *(Hebrew)* Whom God sustains. NOTABLES: Son of Ahab, who ascended to the throne as the eighth king of Israel in 853 B.C. He reigned only two years.

AHIA *(Hebrew)* Brother of Jehovah. NOTABLES: Son of Ahitub and great-grandson of Eli. He was the high priest who brought the Ark of the Covenant to Gibeah (1 Samuel 14:3, 18). VARIATIONS: Achiya, Achiyahu, Ahiah, Ahijah.

AHIMAN *(Egyptian)* Son of Anak. NOTABLES: One of three sons of Anak (the others were Sheshai and Talmai) who were giants and whom Caleb drove out of the city of Hebron (Numbers 13: 33).

AHIMELECH *(Hebrew)* Of the king. NOTABLES: Priest at Nob, son of Ahitub and the younger brother of Ahiah (1 Samuel 14: 3; 1 Samuel 21:1, 22:11).

The Priest Who Helped David and Lost His Life

Ahimelech served as a high priest just as his father, Ahitub, had done years earlier. His father could trace his lineage back to Aaron, the first high priest of the Israelites. When the path of David, son-in-law to King Saul, crossed Ahimelech's, the outcome was disastrous for the priest.

David's popularity had increased while King Saul's had dwindled. The king's jealousy knew no bounds.

He feared David's growing power and intended to eliminate his competition by killing him, his daughter's husband.

Chased by the king and his men, David arrived in Nob at the tabernacle of the Lord where he asked Ahimelech for food. Distressed, he explained to Ahimelech that he was hungry and exhausted. The priest questioned why David had come. David explained that he was there to do the king's business, although it was not the truth.

Ahimelech gave David some shewbread (consecrated bread) to eat since there were no other loaves available. The priest also gave David the sword of Goliath. A spy for Saul reported the meeting to the king. After Saul confronted Ahimelech, he ordered Ahimelech killed for helping David. (1 Samuel 22:16–23)

AHIMOTH *(Hebrew)* Brother of death. Member of the Levite priesthood, son of Elkanah and brother of Amasai (1 Chronicles 6:25).

AHIRA *(Hebrew)* Brother of iniquity; brother of the shepherd. NOTABLES: Son of Enan. Ahira was a prince and belonged to the tribe of Naphtali. He helped in the census-taking during the time that Moses wandered in the wilderness (Numbers 1:15, 2:29, 7:78).

AHIRAM *(Hebrew)* Of a tall man. NOTABLES: The son of Benjamin (Numbers 26:38) VARIATIONS: Aher, Ehi.

AHITUB *(Hebrew)* Of goodness. NOTABLES: Biblical priest whose lineage was through Ithamar, son of Aaron (1 Samuel 14:3).

AHLAI *(Hebrew)* Sweet. NOTABLES: A Biblical man who was in the line from Jacob's son Judah to David (1 Chronicles 2:31).

AKIVA *(Hebrew)* Protect; shelter. VARIATIONS: Akavia, Akaviah, Akavya, Akiba, Kiba, Kiva.

ALBAN *(Latin)* From Alba. VARIATIONS: Albain, Albany, Albean, Albein, Alben.

ALITZ *(Hebrew)* Happy. VARIATIONS: Aliz.

ALLON *(Hebrew)* Oak tree. VARIATIONS: Alon.

AMAHL *(Hebrew)* Hard worker. VARIATIONS: Amal, Amali.

AMALEK *(Arabic)* Dweller in the valley. NOTABLES: Grandson of Esau, the Edomite. Amalek was tribal head of a semi-nomadic people, the Amalekites, who dwelled chiefly in the Negev desert and frequently battled the Israelites (Genesis 36:12). VARIATIONS: Amaleq.

AMASA *(Hebrew)* Hardship. NOTABLES: Son of Abigail, sister of King David and wife of Jether, the Ishmeelite (1 Chronicles 2:13–17). VARIATIONS: Amasai, Amasia, Amasiah, Amasya, Amazu.

AMAZIAH *(Hebrew)* Strengthened by Yahweh. NOTABLES: Son of King Joash and his wife Jehoaddan. Amaziah became the ruler of Judah at the age of twenty-five (2 Kings 14:1–2).

AMBROSE *(Greek)* Immortal being. NOTABLES: Saint Ambrose, Bishop of Milan and Doctor of the Church. VARIATIONS: Ambroce, Ambrus.

AMIEL *(Hebrew)* Lord of the people. NOTABLES: A member of the tribe of Dan and one of Moses' spies sent to scout the land of Canaan (Numbers 13:12). Amiel was also the name of the father of Bathsheba (1 Chronicles 3:5), who married King David. VARIATIONS: Ammiel.

AMON *(Hebrew)* Faithful; true; *(Greek)* builder. NOTABLES: Son of Manasseh, King of Judah, and his wife, Meshullemeth (2 Kings 21:19–20). VARIATIONS: Amen, Ammon, Amoun, Amun, Hammon, Imen, Yamanu.

Amon Reaps What He Sows

When Manasseh, king of Judah, died, his son Amon became king. Amon was twenty-two years old. He steered the Israelites away from worshipping the Hebrew god and moved their hearts and minds once again toward pagan devotion. He sacrificed many animals on the altar of all the false gods, much as his father had done before being seized by the Assyrians and taken to Babylon. Perhaps the greatest difference between Manasseh and Amon was that Amon refused to humble himself before God. Instead, Amon continued to incur the wrath of the Lord. By not admitting his guilt, Amon sealed his fate. His servants plotted against him and took his life. "And the servants of Amon conspired against him, and slew the king in his own house. And the people of the land slew all them that had conspired against king Amon; and the people of the land made Josiah his son king in his stead" (2 Kings 21:23–24).

AMOS *(Hebrew)* Strong one; burden bearer. NOTABLES: Amos was an Old Testament prophet whose story and prophecies are contained in the Bible's book of Amos. VARIATIONS: Amotz, Amoz, Amus.

ANAH *(Hebrew)* Answer. VARIATIONS: Anath.

ANAMIM *(Hebrew)* Flight. NOTABLES: A descendant of Noah in the generations born after the flood (Genesis 10:1–13).

ANANIAS *(Hebrew)* form of Hananiah; Gracious is Yahweh. NOTABLES: Husband of Sapphira, who died after deceiving the Holy Spirit (Acts 5:1-10). Also, a disciple of Jesus whom God told to find Saul of Tarsis and restore his sight (Acts 9:10-19). Also, the name of the priest who heard the Apostle Paul's testimony (Acts 22:5, 23:2).

ANDREW *(English)* Brave and manly. NOTABLES: Disciple of Jesus who was brother of Simon Peter. VARIATIONS: Aindrea, Aindreas, Anders, Andi, Andonis, Andor, Andre, Andreas, Andrei, Andres, Andrey, Andros, Andrzej.

One Who Believed that Jesus Was the Messiah

Andrew and Simon were the sons of Jonas. The men were natives of Bethsaida on the northern shore of the Sea of Galilee but lived in Capernaum, where they worked as fishermen. Andrew was a disciple of John the Baptist (John 1:35–40). After listening to John's teaching about Jesus as the Lamb of God, Andrew believed that Jesus was the Messiah. He introduced his brother Simon to Jesus (John 1:41–42). That was easy enough to do, since at the beginning of Jesus' ministry, the brothers shared the same house in Capernaum. Some time after that, Jesus called upon them to leave their fishing business and become his disciples (Mark 1:16–18).

After Jesus' death, the Apostles took the gospel message to different parts of the world. Peter remained for some time in Jerusalem (before ministering in other places, such as Lydda, Joppa, and the Plain of Sharon) while Andrew spread the gospel message into Asia Minor. Tradition asserts that he was crucified on an X-shaped cross. Throughout the world, this type of cross has become known as the Saint Andrew's Cross. Andrew is the patron saint of Romania and Russia and of the Patriarchate of Constantinople.

ANNAS *(Hebrew)* Form of Ananias. NOTABLES: Father-in-law of Caiaphas, the high priest, who heard testimony from Jesus before turning him over to Pilate (John 18:13).

ANTHONY *(Latin)* Praiseworthy; valuable. NOTABLES: Saint Anthony of Padua. VARIATIONS: Andonios, Andonis, Anntoin, Antin, Antoine, Anton, Antone, Antonello, Antoney, Antoni, Antonin, Antonino, Antonio, Antonius, Antons, Antony, Antos, Tony.

ARCHELAUS *(Latinized from ancient Greek)* The people's master. NOTABLES: One of the sons of Herod the Great. VARIATIONS: Archelaos.

ARD *(Hebrew)* Fugitive. NOTABLES: A Biblical descendant of the tribe of Benjamin, who became the leader of a clan in Egypt (Genesis 46:21). VARIATIONS: Addar, Arden, Ardon, Ardy.

ARELI *(Hebrew)* Lion of God; form of Ariel. NOTABLES: Son of Gad, who accompanied Jacob's people to Egypt (Genesis 46:16).

ARI *(Hebrew)* Lion. Short for Aristotle. VARIATIONS: Arie, Arye.

ARIEL *(Hebrew)* Lion of God. NOTABLES: The man sent to Casiphia by the priest Ezra to find temple workers (Ezra 8:16–17). Casiphia may have been a Babylonian settlement of Levites (the priestly tribe). VARIATIONS: Arel, Ariell, Aryell.

ARIOCH *(Babylonian)* Like a lion. NOTABLES: The man King Nebuchadnezzar ordered to destroy the wise men of Babylon (Daniel 2:24).

ARLES *(Hebrew)* Promise. VARIATIONS: Arlee, Arleigh, Arley, Arlie, Arlis, Arliss, Arly.

ARMON *(Hebrew)* High place. VARIATIONS: Arman, Armen, Armin.

AROD *(Hebrew)* Wild ass. NOTABLES: A member of the family of Arodites (Numbers 26:17). VARIATIONS: Arodi.

ASA *(Hebrew)* Doctor. VARIATIONS: Ase, Aza.

ASHBEL *(Hebrew)* Blame. NOTABLES: One of the sons of Benjamin (Genesis 46:21).

ASHER *(Hebrew)* Fortunate; happy. NOTABLES: Son of Jacob and his wife's maidservant Zilpah. Asher became leader of one of the twelve tribes of Israel (Genesis 30:13). VARIATIONS: Ashur.

ASHKENAZ *(Hebrew)* A son of Gomer. NOTABLES: One of the descendants of Noah (Genesis 10:3) and also the name of a man in the genealogical line from Adam to Jacob (1 Chronicles 1:6). VARIATIONS: Ashchenaz.

ASRIEL *(Hebrew)* Prohibition of God. NOTABLES: The sons of Asriel, the family of the Asrielites, to be counted in the census taken after the plague (Numbers 26:31). VARIATIONS: Ashriel.

AUGUST *(Latin)* Worthy of respect. VARIATIONS: Agostino, Agosto, Aguistin, Agustin, Agustino, Augie, Augustin, Augustine, Augustino, Augusto, Augustus, Augy.

AUGUSTUS *(Latin)* Venerable. NOTABLES: Roman emperor Augustus Caesar.

AURELIUS *(Latin)* Golden. VARIATIONS: Areliano, Aurelio, Aurelo, Auriel.

AVI *(Hebrew)* My God.

AVIDOR *(Hebrew)* Father of a people.

AVIRAM *(Hebrew)* My father is strong. VARIATIONS: Abiram, Avram, Avrom, Avrum.

AVIV *(Hebrew)* Spring.

AVNIEL *(Hebrew)* My God is my strength.

AZARIAH *(Hebrew)* Whom Jehovah aids; helped by Yahweh. NOTABLES: The son of King Jehoram, who succeeded his father as ruler of Judah (2 Chronicles 22:6).

AZRIEL *(Hebrew)* Help from God. NOTABLES: The head of the house of Azriel and a man of valor (1 Chronicles 5:24). VARIATIONS: Aziel, Azrael.

B

BACHIR *(Hebrew)* Oldest son.

BALTHASAR *(Greek)* One of the Three Wise Men, or Magi, of Christmas. VARIATIONS: Balta, Baltazar, Balthazar.

BARABBAS *(Hebrew)* Son of Abba; father's son. NOTABLES: The convict who was freed when Jesus was sentenced to death (Mark 15:7).

BARAK *(Hebrew)* Thunderbolt; lightning. NOTABLES: Military hero who, with Deborah, one of the judges of Israel, won a decisive victory against the Canaanite King Jabin (Judges 4:6). VARIATIONS: Barrak.

BARAM *(Hebrew)* Son of the people.

BARNABAS *(Hebrew)* Comfort. NOTABLES: A Levite named Joseph from Cyprus who was surnamed Barnabas (interpreted as "the son of consolation," Acts 4:36). VARIATIONS: Barnabie, Barnabus, Barnaby, Barnebas, Barney, Barnie, Burnaby.

BARTHOLOMEW *(Hebrew)* Farmer's son. VARIA-TIONS: Bart, Bartek, Bartel, Barth, Barthel, Bar-thelemy, Barthelmy, Barthlomeo, Bartholome, Bartholomieu, Bartoli, Bartolo, Bartolomeo, Bartram.

BARUCH *(Hebrew)* Blessed. NOTABLES: Son of Neriah (Jeremiah 32:12).

BASIL *(Greek)* Royal; kingly. VARIATIONS: Basile, Basilio, Basilios, Basilius, Bazil, Bazyl.

BECHER *(Hebrew)* Firstborn; youth. NOTABLES: Son of Benjamin (Genesis 46:21). VARIATIONS: Beckett.

BELSHAZZAR *(Babylonian)* Baal protect the king. NOTABLES: Son of Nebuchadnezzar and his succes-sor. Belshazzar was king during the period when the Persians and the Medes took Babylon. VARIA-TIONS: Zarek.

A Hand Sent by God Delivers a Message

Belshazzar was the son of King Nebuchadnezzar of Babylonia (although some sources suggest that he may have been the son of Nitocris, daughter of Nebu-chadnezzar). When the king died, Belshazzar became the new monarch. After he had ruled for a time, King Belshazzar desired to throw a large party in order to show off the royal treasures. What had once belonged to his father was under the control of Belshazzar.

The new king's guest list included 1,000 nobles and members of their families. He opened the royal treasury for viewing. Inside, hundreds of beautiful gold and silver goblets gleamed. They had once belonged to the Israelites, but Nebuchadnezzar's men had pillaged the Lord's temple in Jerusalem and had seized them for the Babylonian king.

As his guests sipped their wine from the precious goblets, they praised the gods of gold, silver, wood, bronze, iron, and stone. Until then, Belshazzar had been enjoying the revelry. But then a strange thing happened that struck fear in his heart.

As he sipped his wine and listened to those assembled praise the various gods, a hand appeared in the air before him. Belshazzar trembled. The white incandescent hand wrote words on the wall with only its finger. Then after a few words were written, the hand vanished.

Belshazzar shook uncontrollably. His legs buckled beneath him. His heart pounded. He fell to the ground.

After a short time, when he had recovered from the shock of seeing the glowing, disembodied hand, Belshazzar tried to decipher the words. It appeared that they were written in a strange language that no one present could read. So Belshazzar summoned his wisest men, hoping that they could translate the message for him. He offered great rewards to anyone who could decipher the strange writing. Neither the king, nor his wise men knew if the writing contained an important message or if it was simply scribbling.

Finally Belshazzar's wife, the queen, addressed him. She reminded Belshazzar that there was a wise man in the kingdom whose name was Daniel. He was an Israelite who had once advised Nebuchadnezzar. Belshazzar immediately sent for Daniel.

When Daniel was at last standing before him, Belshazzar asked him if he were indeed the man that his father Nebuchadnezzar had brought from Judah. Satisfied that he was the Israelite endowed with special insights into difficult problems, the king explained the problem to Daniel. He promised Daniel a reward in the form of expensive gifts and promotion to the third highest-ranking ruler in the kingdom if he would interpret the writing. Daniel told him that he had no need of gifts or promotion. He would simply read the writing for the king.

Daniel fell into silence then finally spoke. "Your father," he told Belshazzar, "was a great and powerful king, but the Lord humbled him because of his arrogance." Daniel paused, perhaps to measure his words. "For a while, Nebuchadnezzar was forced to live in exile with the beasts of the wilderness. He finally realized that God's power is greater than that of any earthly king. When he learned that lesson, the Lord returned him to his kingdom and restored his power."

He turned to Belshazzar. "You are a young king. You have never been humbled nor learned the lessons of your father. You oppose the Lord. You drank from the sacred goblets that belong to the Lord's Temple in Jerusalem. While drinking wine from those holy objects, you praised false gods that cannot hear your words of praise. You do not honor the Lord nor do you realize that he holds your lives in his hands. You have asked me to tell you what the hand that the Lord sent has written."

Daniel gazed at the writing and then turned to the king. "The first words written on the wall are *mene, mene, tekel, parsin. Mene* means number, for the Lord has numbered your days. *Tekel* means weighed, for the Lord has weighed your spirit and found it lacking. *Parsin* means divided, for your kingdom will be divided between the Persians and the Medes" (Daniel 5: 25-28).

Belshazzar knew Daniel was right. He ordered a royal robe to be made from the most expensive purple cloth and given to Daniel. He presented Daniel with a golden necklace. He promoted Daniel to the level of third highest ruler in Babylon. Day passed into evening. Sometime during the night, while those within the palace walls slept, Belshazzar was killed. A Mede named Darius assumed the throne to rule Babylon.

BEN *(Hebrew)* Short form of Benjamin.

BENAIAH *(Hebrew)* God builds. VARIATIONS: Benaya, Benayahu.

BENEDICT *(Latin)* Blessed. NOTABLES: Pope Benedict XVI. VARIATIONS: Bence, Benci, Bendek, Bendict, Bendix.

BENJAMIN *(Hebrew)* Son of my right hand; fortunate. NOTABLES: The name of the child that Rachel bore Jacob before dying. She named the newborn Ben-oni but Jacob changed the name to Benjamin (Genesis 35:18). Benjamin became leader of one of the twelve tribes of Israel. VARIATIONS: Ben, Benejamen, Beniamino, Benjaman, Benjamen, Benjamino, Benjamon, Benji, Benjie, Benjiman, Benjimen, Benjy, Bennie, Benny, Minyamin, Minyomei, Minyomi.

BERI *(Hebrew)* Man of the well. NOTABLES: A descendant of Asher (1 Chronicles 7:36, 40).

BERIAH *(Hebrew)* In fellowship; in envy. NOTABLES: The son of Asher (Genesis 46:17; 1 Chronicles 7:31, 40).

BOAZ *(Hebrew)* Quick; swift. NOTABLES: Boaz was the relative of Naomi who became the husband of Ruth, Naomi's widowed daughter-in-law (Ruth 2:1). VARIATIONS: Bo, Boas, Boase, Booz.

BOCHERU *(Hebrew)* The first born. NOTABLES: Azel's son, who was a descendant of King Saul through Jonathan, Saul's son (1 Chronicles 8:38).

BOHAN *(Hebrew)* In them. NOTABLES: A descendant of Reuben. The stone marking the northeastern boundary of Judah and Benjamin was named after Bohan (Joshua 15:6, 18:17).

BOOZ *(Hebrew)* In strength. NOTABLES: A man listed in the genealogy of Jesus as the husband of Ruth, who bore his son Obed (Matthew 1:5). VARIATIONS: Boaz.

BOSOR *(Greek)* Form of Beor; burning; mad; foolish. NOTABLES: Balaam's father (2 Peter 2:15).

BUZI *(Hebrew)* My contempt. NOTABLES: Father of Ezekiel and member of the priestly family of Zadok (Ezekiel 1:3).

C

CAESAR *(Latin)* Majestic ruler. NOTABLES: Surname of the Julian family; identified with four Roman emperors of the New Testament: Caesar Augustus,

Tiberius Caesar, Claudius Caesar, and Nero, whose full name was Nero Claudius Caesar Drusus Germanicus (Luke 2:1, Luke 3:1, Acts 18:2, Acts 25:10–12, respectively).

CAIAPHAS *(possibly Greek form of Qayyafa, from Aramaic)* To raise or set up. NOTABLES: The high priest who met with Jesus after soldiers had brought him from Annas (father-in-law of Caiaphas) to the palace of Caiaphas. The high priest then turned Jesus over to Pilate (John 18:24–28). VARIATIONS: Caiphas.

CAIN *(Hebrew)* Possession. NOTABLES: Adam's son and slayer of his brother Abel (Genesis 4:1). VARIATIONS: Cane, Cayne, Kane.

CALEB *(Hebrew)* Brave or dog; whole-hearted. NOTABLES: One of the spies Joshua had sent to explore the land of Palestine (Joshua 14:6-7). VARIATIONS: Calib, Callob, Chelub, Chelubai, Kaleb.

CAMILLUS *(Latin)* Priest's assistant; servant in the temple.

CANAAN *(Hebrew)* Merchant or trader; name of a land known to the ancient Israelites.

CARMI *(Hebrew)* My vineyard; lamb of the waters. NOTABLES: Son of Reuben (Genesis 46:9).

CEDRON *(Hebrew)* Dark; sad; black. NOTABLES: The name of a brook that Jesus and his disciples stepped over to get into the garden where he prayed until arrested by the soldiers of the chief priests and Pharisees (John 18:1). VARIATIONS: Kedron.

CEPHAS *(Aramaic)* Stone; rock. NOTABLES: Name Jesus gave his disciple Simon Peter (John 1:42).

CHAIM *(Hebrew)* Life. VARIATIONS: Chayim, Haim, Hayim.

CHALIL *(Hebrew)* Flute. VARIATIONS: Halil.

CHENAANAH *(Hebrew)* Broken in pieces. NOTABLES: Father of Zedekiah (1 Kings 22:11). VARIATIONS: Chenani, Chenaniah.

CHESED *(Aramaic)* Destroyer. NOTABLES: Nephew of Abraham, son of Nahor and Milcah (Genesis 22:20–22).

CHILION *(Hebrew)* Complete; perfect. Notables: Ruth's brother-in law, son of Naomi and Elimelech (Ruth 1:2).

CHIRAM *(Hebrew)* Exalted. VARIATIONS: Hiram.

CHRISTIAN *(Greek)* Follower of Christ.

CHRISTOPHER *(Greek)* Christ bearer. NOTABLES: Saint Christopher. VARIATIONS: Chris, Christof, Christofer, Christoff, Christoffer, Christoforus, Christoph, Christophe, Christophoros, Christos, Cris, Cristobal, Cristoforo, Kit, Kitt, Kristofer, Kristofor.

CHUZA *(Greek)* The seer; prophet. NOTABLES: Herod's steward, whose wife was Joanna (Luke 8:3).

CLAUDIUS *(Roman)* Lame. NOTABLES: Roman family name; the Roman emperor whose reign extended from A.D. 41to 54 and whose decree banishing all

Jews from Rome forced Priscilla and Aquila to flee that city (Acts 18:2).

CLEOPHAS *(Hebrew/Latin)* Form of Cleopatros; glory of the father. NOTABLES: Husband of Mary, one of the women who stood at the foot of the cross with Mary, mother of Jesus and Mary Magdalene (John 19:25). VARIATIONS: Cleopas, Clopas.

COZ *(Hebrew)* Son of. NOTABLES: Father of Anub and Zobebah of the family of Aharhel, son of Harum (1 Chronicles 4:8). VARIATIONS: Koz.

CYRENIUS *(Greek)* Warrior; form of Quirinius *(Latin)*. NOTABLES: Grecized name of the Roman governor who conducted the census requiring Joseph and Mary to undertake the trip to Bethlehem that culminated in the birth of Jesus (Luke 2:1–5). VARIATIONS: Quirinius, Quirinus.

CYRUS *(Latin)* Sun.

D

DAGAN *(Hebrew)* Earth. VARIATIONS: Dagon.

DAN *(Hebrew)* A judge. NOTABLES: The son of Jacob and Bilhah, his wife Rachel's handmaiden. Dan became one of the leaders of the twelve tribes of Israel (Genesis 30:4–6).

DANIEL *(Hebrew)* God is my judge. NOTABLES: Biblical Daniel, who was one of the children of Judah and who interpreted King Nebuchadnezzar's dreams (Daniel 2:27–28). VARIATIONS: Dan,

Danakas, Danek, Dani, Daniele, Daniels, Danil, Danila, Danilkar, Danilo, Danko, Dannie, Danniel, Danny, Dano, Danya, Danylets, Danylo, Dasco, Donois, Dusan.

DANNY *(Hebrew)* Short form of Daniel.

DARIUS *(Persian/Greek)* He possesses. NOTABLES: Darius the Mede was the ruler of the Chaldeans (Daniel 9:1).

DATHAN *(Hebrew)* Belonging to a fountain. NOTABLES: A member of the Reubenites who, with his brother Abiram, and Korah, the Levite, rose up against Moses and Aaron in the wilderness and were burned to death in a fire from heaven (Numbers 16:1–3).

DAVID *(Hebrew)* Beloved. NOTABLES: Biblical boy who slew the giant Goliath with a stone (1 Samuel 17:4, 49–50). VARIATIONS: Dave, Daveed, Davi, Davidek, Davie, Davy, Dewey, Dodya.

David Fells the Fiercest Philistine

David, a young shepherd boy from Bethlehem, knew about the Philistine warriors who were enemies of his people, the Jews. But he did not know that one day he would have to fight the fiercest of all the Philistine warriors, a man named Goliath. Goliath wore a coat of mail and a helmet of brass. Brass also protected his legs and his shoulders. The head of his spear weighed "six hundred shekels of iron" (1 Samuel 17:7).

One day the Philistine armies had gathered at Shochoh, a place in Judah. They were camped on one mountain and across the valley on the other mountain the armies of King Saul had assembled. On that day, Goliath called out to the Israelites, "Why are ye come out to set your battle in array? Am not I a Philistine, and ye servants to Saul? Choose you a man for you, and let him come down to me" (1 Samuel 17:8). The fight would end in the death of either the Philistine or the Israelite and would settle which would be the victor and which the vanquished.

David was the son of Jesse the Ephrathite of Bethlehem. He joined his three brothers, Eliab, Abinadab, and Shammah, in following Saul's armies against the Philistines. But David, being the youngest, had to leave at the end of the day and return to Bethlehem to feed his father's sheep. The next morning, he left early loaded with loaves of bread and cheese given to him by his father for Saul and his men. While talking with the soldiers, Goliath, the Philistine of Gath, approached and reissued his challenge. The men of Saul's armies greatly feared the giant. Who among them could win a fight with such a warrior?

David offered his services to the king. But Saul pointed out that he was only a youth and Goliath was a veteran soldier. David persisted. Saul relented. He gave the boy his own armor, helmet, a coat of mail, and a sword. David, however, refused them. He pulled forth his sling and chose five smooth stones from the brook flowing nearby. Goliath, with a man armed with shield and sword in front of him, approached. When he saw that the Israelites had put a boy forth to fight him, he cursed.

But David had the God of Abraham on his side and a pretty good aim. He sized up Goliath, took his best shot, and the mighty Philistine fell. His accomplishment earned David high praise and honor by his people and struck fear in the heart of enemies of the Jews.

DEKER *(Hebrew)* To pierce.

DIKLAH *(Hebrew/Aramaic)* Palm Grove.

DODANIM *(Hebrew)* Beloved. NOTABLES: One of the descendants of Noah born after the flood (Genesis 10:4).

DOV *(Hebrew)* Bear.

E

EBENEZER *(Hebrew)* Rock foundation. VARIATIONS: Ebbaneza, Eben, Ebeneezer, Ebeneser, Ebenezar.

EFRAIN *(Hebrew)* Fruitful. VARIATIONS: Efran, Efrane, Efren.

EHI *(Hebrew)* Form of Ahiram.

EITAN *(Hebrew)* Form of Ethan. VARIATIONS: Eithan, Eiton.

ELAM *(Hebrew)* Highland.

ELAN *(Hebrew)* Tree. VARIATIONS: Ilan.

ELDAD *(Hebrew)* God has loved.

ELEAZAR *(Hebrew)* God helps. VARIATIONS: Eliazar, Eliezer.

EPHRON *(Hebrew)* Singing bird. VARIATIONS: Efran, Efrin, Efron, Efroni.

ELI *(Hebrew)* God is great. VARIATIONS: Elie, Ely.

ELIAKIM *(Hebrew)* God raises up.

ELIAZ *(Hebrew)* My God is powerful. VARIATIONS: Elias.

ELIHU *(Hebrew)* Yahweh is my God. NOTABLES: Son of Barachel, a distant relative of Abraham who sat with Job and raised the discussion to new levels of inspiration and insight. He urged Job to be positive and think about the miracles and wonders shown by God (Job 37:14).

ELIJAH *(Hebrew)* The Lord is my God. NOTABLES: Old Testament prophet (1 Kings 17:1-2).VARIATIONS: Elek, Elias, Eliasz, Elie, Eliya, Eliyahu, Ellis, Elya.

Elijah Challenges Ahab and the Prophets of Baal

Elijah was an Old Testament Hebrew prophet who lived during the reign (circa 875 to 850 B.C.) of Ahab. King Ahab had married Jezebel, daughter of the king of Tyre. His marriage to her strengthened his alliance with Phoenicia and fostered widespread cult worship of the pagan god Baal. At a time when the people of the northern kingdom of Israel followed the worship practice of their king and queen, Elijah increasingly was having to remind the Israelites that their worship should remain focused on the Lord God of Abraham regardless of what their royal leaders were doing.

King Ahab decided to erect an altar to Baal in Samaria, a city in the northern kingdom. Omri, Ahab's father, had purchased the hill for two talents of silver with the hope of using the location as his seat of power. He renamed the place Samaria, after the man from whom he purchased the land, and Samaria eventually became a thriving city and capital of the northern kingdom. It was there that Ahab put up an altar in the house of Baal. "And Ahab made a grove; and Ahab did more to provoke the Lord God of Israel to anger than all the kings of Israel that were before him" (1 Kings 16:32–33).

A drought parched the land for three years. During the terrible drought Elijah was sustained with bread and water from a widow whose child he had saved. During the drought's third year, Elijah received divine inspiration that he should go and confront Ahab. During the drought, the king had busied himself trying to find substantial water and food for his livestock while his wife Jezebel arranged to have numerous Hebrew prophets murdered. Obadiah, one of Ahab's military officers who had remained loyal to the Hebrew prophets, arranged a meeting between the king and Elijah. The king wasted no time accusing Elijah of bringing the drought upon Israel. Elijah responded that the drought was caused by Ahab's worship of Baal. By worshipping Baal, the king had broken the first of God's Ten Commandments. Elijah proposed a face-off between himself and the priests of Baal.

On the appointed day, they met on Mount Carmel. Four hundred and fifty prophets of Baal and four hundred prophets of Ashera, the female deity worshipped by Jezebel, showed up to meet Elijah. The people of

Israel gathered to watch. The prophets of Baal made a sacrifice to their god, asking that the sacrifice might burst into flames to become a burnt offering. For hours, they cut themselves and cried out for Baal to ignite the wood, but there was no answer and no sign that their voices had been heard.

As evening gathered, Elijah took twelve stones, representing the twelve tribes of Israel, and built an altar. He piled up the wood and drenched it in water poured from no less than four barrels. He made a trench to run around the altar and filled the trench with water. He laid out bullock meat for a sacrifice and called upon the Lord God to ignite the fire and burn the offering. "Then the fire of the Lord fell, and consumed the burnt sacrifice, and the wood, and the stones, and the dust, and licked up the water that was in the trench. And when all the people saw it, they fell on their faces: and they said, "The Lord, he is the God; the Lord, he is the God" (1 Kings 18:38–39).

A victorious Elijah had the prophets of Baal gathered together and taken to the brook Kishon where they were slain. To Ahab, he said "Get thee up, eat, and drink; for there is a sound of abundance of rain" (1 Kings 18:41). Indeed, the heavens went black and the clouds appeared, blown by the wind, and a great rain fell over the land. "And the hand of the Lord was on Elijah; and he girded up his loins, and ran before Ahab to the entrance of Jezreel" (1 Kings 18:46).

ELIRAN *(Hebrew)* My God is song. VARIATIONS: Eliron.

ELISHA *(Hebrew)* God is my salvation. NOTABLES: Prophet of the Old Testament (1 Kings 19:16). VARIATIONS: Elish, Elisher, Elishua.

ELIUD *(Hebrew)* God of Judah. NOTABLES: Hebrew man who is included in the genealogy of Jesus from Abraham (Matthew 1:14).

ELIYAHU *(Hebrew)* The Lord is my God.

ELKANAH *(Hebrew)* He whom God possessed. NOTABLES: Israelite who was named among those Moses led out of Egypt (Exodus 6:24); husband of Hannah and father of the Old Testament prophet Samuel (1 Samuel 1:1–2, 20).

ELNATHAN *(Hebrew)* The Lord has given. NOTABLES: King Jehoiachin's grandfather (2 Kings 24:8).

ELON *(Hebrew)* Oak. NOTABLES: Esau married Judith, the daughter of Beeri, a Hittite, and Bashemath, who was the daughter of Elon, also a Hittite (Genesis 26:34).

ELZAPHAN *(Hebrew)* Whom God protects. NOTABLES: Biblical son of Uzziel (Exodus 6: 22; Leviticus 10:4; Numbers 3:30). VARIATIONS: Elizaphan.

EMMANUEL *(Hebrew)* God is with us. NOTABLES: Jesus (Matthew 1:23). VARIATIONS: Emanuel, Emmanuil, Immanuel, Manny, Manuel.

EMMOR *(Greek)* Form of Hammor. NOTABLES: Father of Sychem, whose sons sold Abraham a tomb (Acts 7:16).

ENOCH *(Hebrew)* Dedicated; experienced. NOTABLES: Son of Cain, who lived 365 years and walked with God (Genesis 4:17).

ENOS *(Hebrew)* Man. NOTABLES: Seth's son and grandson of Adam and Eve (Genesis 4:26). VARIATIONS: Enosa, Enosh.

EPHRAIM *(Hebrew)* Fruitful; fertile. NOTABLES: The son that Asenath, daughter of Potipherah, priest of On, bore to Joseph (Genesis 41:50–52). VARIATIONS: Efraim, Efrain, Efrayim, Efrem, Efren, Ephraim, Ephrain, Ephrayim.

EPHRON *(Hebrew)* Like a fawn. NOTABLES: Son of Zohar, the Hittite, owner of the field and the cave that Abraham bought as a place to bury his wife Sarah (Genesis 23:8–20).

ER *(Hebrew)* Watchful. NOTABLES: Son of Judah (one of the sons of Jacob) and Shuah, a Canaanite woman (Genesis 38:2–3). VARIATIONS: Eri.

ERAN *(Hebrew)* Watchful. NOTABLES: Grandson of Ephraim (Numbers 26:36).

ERASTUS *(Greek)* Beloved. NOTABLES: One of two men that the Apostle Paul sent to Macedonia while he stayed in Asia (Acts 19:22).

ESARHADDON *(Assyrian)* Ashur has given me a brother. NOTABLES: Son of Assyrian king Sennacherib, who succeeded Sennacherib as king (2 Kings 19:36–37). His rule extended from 680 to 669 B.C. VARIATIONS: Ashur-aha-iddina.

ESAU *(Hebrew)* Rough and hairy. NOTABLES: Son of Rebekah and Isaac, brother of Jacob (Genesis 25:25–26).

Esau Tricked Out of His Birthright

Esau and Jacob could not be more different. Esau had emerged from his mother's womb red-colored. He was hairy, enjoyed the outdoors, and was an expert hunter who often brought home venison that his father Isaac loved to eat. His brother Jacob's skin was fair and smooth. Jacob was not a great hunter or outdoorsman. He was a man of softer temperament than the burly Esau. Perhaps because Rebekah loved Jacob more or worried that he would not do as well in life as his accomplished brother, she developed a plan to rob Esau of the blessing of the eldest son and ensure that Jacob, instead, received it.

When Isaac was close to dying, he called Esau to his side and told him that he wanted some venison. Upon Esau's return, he was to make a meal of it for the old man. After Isaac ate, he would then bless Esau and die in peace. Esau immediately left to do his father's bidding. Before Esau could return, however, Rebekah, who had overheard the exchange between father and son, told Jacob to put goatskins upon his hands and take in some savory venison that she had just prepared. He was to pretend he was Esau and ask for the blessing of the firstborn. The blessing was the way sons received the inheritance of fields, animals, and wealth of their fathers.

The goatskin tied onto Jacob's hands convinced the aging Isaac that he was indeed with his eldest son Esau. He ate the venison stew that Jacob offered and then pronounced the blessing upon Jacob as if he were saying the words in the presence of Esau.

When Esau returned and discovered the ruse, he let go a great and bitter cry, saying, "Bless me, even me also, O my father" (Genesis 27:34). But the deed had been done and could not be reversed.

Esau hated Jacob. He vowed to mourn the death of his father when Isaac passed away. But then, when the time was right, he would murder his brother. Rebekah learned about Esau's plan, so she told Jacob to flee to the safety of her brother's home. But before she let him go, she complained to Isaac that she did not want Jacob to marry any of the women of Heath. So Isaac counseled Jacob to take a wife from among the daughters of Laban, Rebekah's brother.

For a long time, the relationship between Jacob and Esau remained estranged. Both took wives and had children. Esau first married Canaanite women but later took Mahalath, the daughter of Ishmael, as a wife. Esau's descendants were known as the Edomites. Eventually, he and Jacob reconciled.

ESROM *(Hebrew)* Enclosed wall; form of Hezron.

ETHAN *(Hebrew)* Steadfast. VARIATIONS: Eathan, Ethe, Ethen.

EUTYCHUS *(Latin)* Fortunate. NOTABLES: The young man whom the Apostle Paul raised from the dead (Acts 20:9–12).

EZBON *(Hebrew)* Hastening to understand. NOTABLES: One of the sons of Gad (Genesis 46:16) and also one of the sons of Bela, grandson of Benjamin (1 Chronicles 7:7).

EZEKIEL *(Hebrew)* The strength of God. VARIATIONS: Ezekial, Ezequiel, Zeke.

EZRA *(Hebrew)* Helper. NOTABLES: Son of Seraiah and a scribe in the law of Moses (Ezra 7:6). VARIATIONS: Esra, Ezera, Ezri.

F

FRANCIS *(Latin)* Frenchman.

G

GABE *(Hebrew)* Short form of Gabriel.

GABRIEL *(Hebrew)* Man of God. NOTABLES: Angel who appeared to the Virgin Mary to announce the forthcoming birth of Jesus (Luke 1:26–27) and also appeared to Zechariach, husband of Elizabeth, the Virgin Mary's cousin, to announce the birth of John the Baptist (Luke 1:11–12). VARIATIONS: Gab, Gabby, Gabe, Gabi, Gabko, Gabo, Gabor, Gabriele, Gabrielli, Gabriello, Gabris, Gabys, Gavi, Gavriel.

GAD *(Hebrew)* A troop cometh. NOTABLES: Son of Jacob and Zilpah, handmaiden to Jacob's wife Leah. Gad became the leader of one of the twelve tribes of Israel (Genesis 30:9–11).

GAMLIEL *(Hebrew)* God is my reward. VARIATIONS: Gamaliel.

GAVRIEL *(Hebrew)* God is my strength; God is my might.

GEHAZI *(Hebrew)* Valley of vision. NOTABLES: Trusted servant of the prophet Elisha (2 Kings 4:12).

Gehazi Stricken with Leprosy for His Duplicitous Behavior

Gehazi, faithful servant to the prophet Elisha, wasn't a bad man. He just had a weakness when it came to money in his own pocket.

Word had traveled beyond Israel in ancient times that the Hebrew prophet Elisha had performed certain miracles. Most recently, people talked about how he revived the dead child of a certain Shunemite woman.

The Bible doesn't say whether or not Gehazi ever knew Naaman, captain of the king of Syria's military forces, but their paths were destined to cross. Naaman suffered from leprosy. His wife's servant had heard the stories circulating about the healing powers of the prophet Elisha. The servant knew that her mistress fretted about her husband's incurable skin condition. Perhaps Elisha could help. Naaman's wife persuaded him to make a request of the king to allow Naaman to go and find Elisha.

The King of Syria wanted his captain to become healthy and gladly sent Naaman into Israel with a letter to the Israelite king asking him to help to heal

Naaman of his leprosy. He also sent "ten talents of silver, and six thousand pieces of gold, and ten changes of raiment" (2 Kings 5:5).

The King of Israel, fearing that the King of Syria was trying to provoke an argument, tore his clothes and asked, "Am I God, to kill and to make alive, that his man doth send unto me to recover a man of his leprosy?" (2 Kings 5:7)

When Elisha heard that his king had become so distressed, he sent word to the king to redirect Naaman to his house. When Naaman arrived, Elisha told him to go wash in the river Jordan seven times. But Naaman thought that the simple act of washing in the river was not going to cure him. And why weren't the rivers in Syria as good as the Jordan for washing one's body? Naaman left, enraged.

It was left to Naaman's servant to coax him into doing as the prophet Elisha had instructed. Naaman finally went into the river and dipped seven times. His flesh became like that of a newborn child. He returned to Elisha with his entire company and offered Elisha all the wealth that he had brought from Syria, but the prophet refused. It was enough that Naaman had sworn that one true god was the God of Israel.

So Naaman left, and shortly thereafter, Elisha's servant Gehazi left, too. When Naaman spotted Gehazi running after him, he pulled his chariot to a halt and dropped to the ground to ask Gehazi if all was well.

Gehazi told Naaman that Elisha, his master, had sent him. Gehazi explained that two young followers of the prophet had just come and Gehazi would like to take to them a talent of silver and two changes of garments. Naaman agreed and handed them over. When Gehazi had returned to Elisha's house, the prophet wanted to know where he had been. Gehazi lied and said he hadn't gone anywhere. The prophet Elisha knew he was lying and so pronounced a curse, "The leprosy therefore of Naaman shall cleave unto thee, and unto thy seed forever" (2 Kings 5:27).

GERA *(Hebrew)* A grain, as a measurement. VARIATIONS: Gerah.

GERSHON *(Hebrew)* Exiled. VARIATIONS: Gershom, Gerson.

GIANNI *(Italian)* Short form of Giovanni (John). VARIATIONS: Giannes, Giannos.

GIBBAR *(Hebrew)* Hero.

GIDEON *(Hebrew)* One who cuts down trees, a logger. VARIATIONS: Gideone, Gidon, Gidoni.

GILAM *(Hebrew)* Joy of a people.

GILBEAH *(Hebrew)* Hill.

GILBOAH *(Hebrew)* Pouring forth, bubbling fountain.

GILEAD *(Arabic)* Camel's hump. VARIATIONS: Gilad, Giladi.

GIPSA *(Hebrew)* Flattery.

GOLIATH *(Hebrew)* Exiled. NOTABLES: Philistine warrior slain by the shepherd boy David with his slingshot (1 Samuel 17:4). VARIATIONS: Golliath.

GOMER *(Hebrew)* Complete. NOTABLES: One of the sons of Japheth born after the flood (Genesis 10:2).

GREGORY *(Latin)* Observant. VARIATIONS: Greg, Gregg, Gregoire, Gregor, Gregorio, Gregorios, Gregos, Greig, Gries, Grigor.

GUNI *(Hebrew)* Painted with colors. NOTABLES: A descendant of Rachel and Jacob (Genesis 46:22–24).

H

HADAD *(Arabic)* The Syrian god of virility.

HAGGI *(Hebrew)* Festive. NOTABLES: One of the sons of Gad (Genesis 46:16). VARIATIONS: Haggai.

HAM *(Hebrew)* Heat. Short form of Hamilton. NOTABLES: One of the sons of Noah (Genesis 10:1).

The Tower of Babel: A Story of Ham

Noah had three sons—Ham, Shem, and Japheth. Each son grew into manhood and took a wife. Their wives gave them many children, so many that each brother started a kingdom with his own family or tribe of people. The people in each kingdom had families and their families continued to increase in size. Although people did not know it, God's plan was for them to travel far and wide and settle in many lands in order to fill the world. Since everyone was a descendant of

Noah, the people saw themselves as members of one family. They lived in peace. They spoke one language.

About a hundred years after the Deluge, a group of people settled upon a fertile plain in the kingdom of Shinar. The group split itself into tribes and the tribes pushed into new territories. These nomadic tent people realized that it was becoming difficult to find each other.

The tribal leaders joined together in an effort to figure out a plan to keep everyone connected. They finally decided to erect a great city in the field. At dead center, they would build a tower that would project upward into the sky, perhaps all the way to heaven. People everywhere would be able to see the tower. Soon, construction began with the making of bricks out of mud and straw. For mortar, the people used asphalt from the sea.

One day God surveyed the building of the tower. He observed that the people were all speaking one language and working together. United in mind and purpose, humanity showed that they could accomplish anything they desired. They did not seek God's guidance. God had a different purpose for humanity. He went down to the city to confound their language so that the tribes would not understand one another's speech. When tribal members could not speak and understand the same language, they abandoned the building of the tower and set off to settle the lands of the world. The city became known as Babel and the tower was called the Tower of Babel. Work on the structure was never completed. Tradition states that the tower toppled when the Lord brought a powerful wind against it.

HAMAL *(Arabic)* Lamb.

HAMOR *(Greek)* Donkey; clay; dirt. **NOTABLES:** The man who owned the parcel of ground in Shechem that Jacob purchased from the man's sons (Joshua 24:32).

HANAN *(Hebrew)* God is good; God is gracious.

HANANIAH *(Hebrew)* Gracious is the Lord. **NOTABLES:** Name of several men in the Old Testament, including the father of Zedekiah during the reign of King Jehoiakim of Judah (Jeremiah 36:12).

HAREL *(Hebrew)* Mountain of God. **VARIATIONS:** Harell, Harrell.

HASKEL *(Hebrew)* Wisdom. **VARIATIONS:** Chaskel, Haskell, Heskel.

HAVILAH *(Hebrew)* Stretch of sand. **NOTABLES:** Son of Cush (Genesis 10:7); also son of Joktan (Genesis 10:29). Finally, a place name in the Old Testament (Genesis 2:11).

HAZAEL *(Hebrew)* He whom God watches over; God sees. **NOTABLES:** The man whom God told the prophet Elijah to anoint as the future king of Syria (1 Kings 19:15).

HEBER *(Hebrew)* Form of Eber. **NOTABLES:** Generations of a family in the genealogy of Noah's descendants born after the flood (Genesis 10:21).

HEBRON *(Hebrew)* Alliance.

HELI *(Greek)* A form of the name Eli. NOTABLES: Name of the father of Joseph, who was Mary's husband and Jesus' stepfather (Luke 3:23).

HEROD *(Greek)* Hero's song. NOTABLES: Herod the Great and Herod Antipas are two Herods who are mentioned in the New Testament Gospels of Matthew, Mark, Luke, and John. Herod the Great ruled over ancient Israel during the time of Jesus' birth. When he died, the Roman Emperor Augustus divided Israel between three of Herod's sons. One of them, Herod Antipas, become tetrarch of Galilee during Jesus' lifetime (Luke 3:1) and played a pivotal role in the final judgment and subsequent death of Jesus.

HEZEKIAH *(Hebrew)* God gives strength. NOTABLES: Ruler of Judah who fought the Assyrians and the Philistines.

Hezekiah Fights the Assyrian King

Hezekiah, an Israelite king who ruled from 726 to 697 B.C. over the southern kingdom of Judah, implored his people to worship God and to follow the Ten Commandments. Long before he ruled over Judah, land occupied by the Hebrews had been ruled over by David and Solomon. Then it had been divided into two kingdoms. Ten tribes formed the Northern Kingdom called Israel. The Southern Kingdom, formed by the tribes of Judah and Benjamin, was called Judah. Some of the nineteen kings who had ruled over the Northern Kingdom had adopted pagan worship.

The kings of the Southern Kingdom mainly served God, but even the Southern Kingdom people had begun to venerate idols. Israel and Judah became increasingly weaker. Hezekiah destroyed the idols in Judah in an effort to turn the hearts and minds of his people back to the worship of God.

Meanwhile, King Sennacherib of Assyria decided to invade the lands occupied by the Israelites. Border skirmishes and confrontations began and continued until Sennacherib's army launched its assault. Sennacherib brought in non-Hebrews to resettle in Samaria, the administrative capital, as well as other cities and towns.

Hezekiah knew that the Assyrian army was formidable and that his people could not withstand a full-blown invasion. He sent word to Sennacherib that he would pay any price to have the Assyrians leave. Sennacherib demanded excessive quantities of gold and silver. Hezekiah did the unthinkable—stripped the gold from the interior of Solomon's temple in Jerusalem. He gave it to the Assyrian king (2 Kings:14–15).

Sennacherib finally had all the gold and silver from the Jews in hand. He sent an army to Jerusalem. His soldiers shouted to the Jews to surrender and taunted the Israelites.

Hezekiah prayed to the God of Abraham, begging his divine Father for deliverance. His prayer was answered in the form of an angel of death who "went out, and smote in the camp of the Assyrians a hundred fourscore and five thousand: and when they arose early in the morning, behold, they were all dead corpses" (2 Kings 19:35).

The Assyrian king surveyed the bodies and retreated to Nineveh. As he worshipped his pagan god, his own sons "smote him with the sword: and they escaped into the land of Armenia. And Esarhaddon, his son, reigned in his stead" (2 Kings 19:37).

Some time after the Assyrian king's retreat, Hezekiah became gravely ill. The prophet Isaiah, son of Amoz, went to the king and told him to get his affairs straight, for his death was near. Hezekiah began to pray, reminding the Lord that he had walked "before thee in truth and with a perfect heart, and have done that which is good in thy sight (2 Kings 20:3). As the king wept, Isaiah departed.

The prophet had gone only a short distance before the Word of God came to him that he should return to the king. Isaiah told Hezekiah that his prayers had been heard. The Lord would now add fifteen years to his life. Isaiah told Hezekiah to take a lump of figs and boil them. Thereafter he would recover.

Hezekiah, relieved, asked for a sign that his prophecy would come true. Isaiah told the king to watch the sundial's shadow. When the shadow moved backward ten degrees instead of forward, Hezekiah could take it as a sign of God's promise. Hezekiah did indeed live another fifteen years.

HEZRON *(Hebrew)* Enclosed wall. NOTABLES: A descendant of Jacob when he and his people went into Egypt (Genesis 46:8–12). VARIATIONS: Ezron, Hezrai.

HILLEL *(Hebrew)* Highly praised.

HIRAH *(Hebrew)* Nobility.

HIRAM *(Hebrew)* Most noble man. VARIATIONS: Hirom, Hyrum.

HODIAH *(Hebrew)* God is great. VARIATIONS: Hodia, Hodiya.

HONORE *(Latin)* Honored.

HOSEA *(Hebrew)* Salvation.

HUPPIM *(Hebrew)* Form of Hupham; inhabitant of the shore. NOTABLES: One of the sons of Benjamin (Genesis 46:21). VARIATIONS: Hupham.

HUSHAM *(Hebrew)* Haste. NOTABLES: the name of the man in the land of Temani who reigned after Jobab died (Genesis 36:34).

I

ICHABOD *(Hebrew)* The glory is no more. VARIATIONS: Ikabod, Ikavod.

IDAN *(Hebrew)* Era.

IGNATIUS *(English)* Fervent; on fire. NOTABLES: Saint Ignatius of Loyola. VARIATIONS: Iggy, Ignac, Ignace, Ignacek, Ignacio, Ignatious, Ignatz, Ignaz, Ignazio, Inigo, Nacek, Nacicek.

IRIJAH *(Hebrew)* Whom Jehovah looks upon. NOTABLES: The sentry who arrested the prophet Jeremiah (Jeremiah 37:13).

ISAAC *(Hebrew)* Laughter. NOTABLES: Son of Abraham and Sarah whom God used to test the faith of the patriarch Abraham (Genesis 22:6). VARIATIONS: Isaak, Isak, Itzak, Ixaka, Izaak.

Finding the Perfect Wife for Isaac

Abraham's wife, Sarah, passed away before Isaac, their son, had taken a suitable wife. Abraham desired his son to marry from among the Hebrews living in the land of his birth rather than in Canaan where they had made their home for many years. Since Abraham was too old and feeble to travel, he sent his most trusted and faithful servant to find a suitable woman from among his people.

The servant asked what he should do if she refused to return with him to Canaan. Should he take Isaac to meet her? Abraham said that under no circumstances was Isaac to leave Canaan. Abraham told his servant that God had promised to give Canaanite land to his descendants and, therefore, Isaac had to remain where he was. Abraham explained that if the servant found such a woman from among his people and she refused to return to meet Isaac, then Abraham would release the servant from his oath.

The servant undertook the journey to Nahor, in Mesopotamia, the place Abraham was born. Ten large camels bore the treasures he took with him. The servant guided the camels to the well beyond the city. It was already late in the day and women were in line with their water jugs.

The servant of Abraham and his camels were thirsty. He said a prayer to the Lord, asking that "the damsel to whom I shall say, Let down thy pitcher, I pray thee, that I may drink; and she shall say, Drink, and I will give thy camels drink also; let the same be she that thou hast appointed for thy servant Isaac; and thereby shall I know that thou hast shewed kindness unto my master" (Genesis 24:14).

He had barely finished his prayer when a beautiful young woman named Rebekah, a relative of Abraham's brother, approached carrying on her shoulder a large jug of water. The servant asked her for a drink to quench his thirst.

Although the jug was heavy to hoist up and down off her shoulder, Rebekah readily complied with the stranger's request. "Drink, my lord," Rebekah told him. "And when she had done giving him drink, she said, I will draw water for thy camels also" (Genesis 24:18–19). She poured her pitcher of water into the trough for the camels and returned to the well to draw up another bucket of water to replenish her pitcher.

Abraham's servant pulled from his bag a nose ring and two gold bracelets and presented them to her. He inquired about her parents. She told him that she was the daughter of Bethuel, Nahor's son. Nahor was Abraham's brother. She insisted that the servant spend the night in her family's large home. They even had room for the camels. Rebekah hurried home to tell her family about their guest. Abraham's servant fell to his knees and offered thanks to God. This surely was the woman the Lord had chosen for Isaac's wife.

Laban, Rebekah's brother, saw her new jewelry. He rushed to the well to meet the servant of Abraham and invited him to stay with his family.

Abraham's servant explained his purpose. He asked Laban and Bethuel if Rebekah could return with him to marry Isaac. They answered that it was the will of God. The servant thanked Bethuel and gave him all of the treasures he had brought.

Early the next day, the servant and Rebekah set out for Canaan. She was eager to meet her new husband and see her new home. They arrived as Isaac was in the field praying. Rebekah covered herself with a veil.

Isaac and Rebekah married and began living in the tent of his mother Sarah and his father Abraham. The Lord blessed their match and love grew strong between them. "Isaac was comforted after his mother's death" (Genesis 24:67).

ISAIAH *(Hebrew)* God helps me. Notable: The Old Testament prophet who lived approximately 700 years before the birth of Christ and who began his work as a prophet during the reign of Uzziah, king of Judea (Isaiah 1:1).

ISHMAEL *(Hebrew)* God that hears; may God hear. NOTABLES: Son of Abraham and Hagar, his wife Sarah's maidservant.

Ishmael and His Children

Until the age of fourteen, Ishmael had the full attention of his father Abraham. But then, Isaac was born to his father's wife, Sarah. With the arrival of her own son, Sarah asked Abraham to send away Ishmael and Hagar, Ishmael's mother. It clearly hurt Abraham to do so, but he provided for them and sent them into the wilderness. Abraham had another concubine named Keturah and had sons by her as well. When

Abraham died, his sons Ishmael and Isaac, by then grown with families of their own, attended to his burial. The patriarch of the Hebrews was placed in the cave of Machpelah where Abraham had buried Sarah (Genesis 25:8–10).

When Ishmael married, his mother Hagar chose for him an Egyptian wife. He fathered twelve sons and a daughter. He named his girl Mahalath (Genesis 28:9). Elsewhere in the book of Genesis, the name is spelled Bashemath (Genesis 36:3). Ishmael named his sons Nebajoth, Kedar, Adbeel, Mibsam, Mishma, Dumah, Massa, Hadar, Tema, Jetur, Naphish, Kedemah (Genesis 25:13–15). His people became known as the Ishmaelites. Ishmael lived to be one hundred and thirty-seven.

ISRAEL *(Hebrew)* Upright with God; struggle with God. NOTABLES: The new name God gave the Hebrew patriarch Jacob (Genesis 35:10). VARIATIONS: Yisrael.

ISSACHAR *(Hebrew)* Man for hire. NOTABLES: Son of Jacob and his wife Leah. Issachar became a leader of one of the twelve tribes of Israel (Genesis 30:18).

ISUAH *(Hebrew)* Level.

ITHAMAR *(Hebrew)* Island of palms. NOTABLES: Biblical son born to Aaron by Elisheba (Exodus 6:23).

ITZHAK *(Hebrew)* Form of Isaac. VARIATIONS: Yitzhak.

IZEHAR *(Hebrew)* Oil.

IZZY *(Hebrew)* Short form of Isaac.

J

JABEZ *(Hebrew)* Born in pain. VARIATIONS: Jabes, Jabesh, Jabus.

JABIN *(Hebrew)* God has created.

JACHAN *(Hebrew)* Troubled.

JACOB *(Hebrew)* Supplanter; heel. VARIATIONS: Jaco, Jacobus, Jacoby, Jacquet, Jakab, Jake, Jakie, Jakiv, Jakob, Jakov, Jakub, Jakubek, Kiva, Kivi.

JAHLEEL *(Hebrew)* Hoping in God. NOTABLES: Biblical sons and descendants of the Jahleelites (Numbers 26:26).

JAIRUS *(Hebrew)* God clarifies; my light; who diffuses light. NOTABLES: The man whose dying daughter was revived by Jesus (Mark 5:22–23).

Jesus Raises the Daughter of Jairus

Jairus was a leader in the synagogue in Capernaum. One day a large crowd awaited the arrival of a boat bearing Jesus. As Jesus climbed off the boat, the crowd that had gathered in anticipation of his arrival surged forward. Jairus was among them. He fell at Jesus' feet and asked Jesus to go with him to his house. Jairus had a twelve-year-old daughter. She was so ill that she was not expected to survive. Like any father, Jairus felt desperate and would do anything to save his child. His faith was great that the preacher whom many called the Messiah could save her.

On the way to the house of Jairus, the people pressed in upon them. Jesus' disciples walked along with Jesus and Jairus but none of them saw the woman who touched the hem of Jesus' robe.

The unseen woman had had a blood issue problem for twelve years. No one had been able to help her. But her faith in Jesus was so great that she believed if she simply touched his clothing, she would be healed. Indeed, she was.

Jesus knew someone in that crowd had touched him and, to the surprise of his disciples, he asked who it was. The woman stepped forward and confessed. Jesus told her, "Daughter, thy faith hath made thee whole; go in peace, and be whole of thy plague" (Mark 5:34).

During the exchange between Jesus and the woman, Jairus was told that his daughter had died. Jesus hastened to the house, allowing only his closest disciples, Peter, James, and his brother John, to accompany him. Already the house was filled the sounds of great wailing. Jesus said, "Why make ye this ado, and weep? The damsel is not dead, but sleepeth" (Mark 5:39).

He went into the room where the girl lay. He took her by the hand and in his Aramaic language spoke the words "Talitha cumi; which is, being interpreted, Damsel, I say unto thee, arise" (Mark 5:41). And she arose and walked. Jesus instructed those present to give her something to eat.

JAMES *(Hebrew)* The one who replaces; disciple of Jesus. NOTABLES: An important figure in the Jerusalem community of Jesus' followers. Also, the name of the disciple who was the brother of John.

The sons of Zebedee, James and John were also called Boanerges, or the "sons of thunder" (Mark 3:17) VARIATIONS: Jaymes, Jim, Jimmy. .

JAMIN *(Hebrew)* Favored one.

JAPHETH *(Hebrew)* He increases. VARIATIONS: Jafet, Japeth, Japhet.

JARAH *(Hebrew)* Sweet.

JAREB *(Hebrew)* One who is contentious; he struggles.

JARED *(Hebrew)* Descend. VARIATIONS: Jarad, Jarid, Jarod, Jarrad, Jarred, Jerad, Jered, Jerod, Jerrad, Jerrod, Jerryd, Yarden, Yared.

JARON *(Hebrew)* To sing or shout. VARIATIONS: Gerron, Jaran, Jaren, Jarin, Jarran, Jarren, Jarron, Jeran, Jeren, Jeron, Jerrin, Jerron, Yaron.

JASON *(Graeco-Judean)* Equivalent of Joshua; God is my salvation. VARIATIONS: Jacen, Jaison, Jase, Jasen, Jayce, Jaycen, Jaysen, Jayson.

JAVAN *(Hebrew)* Son of Biblical Japheth. VARIATIONS: Javin, Javon.

JEB *(Hebrew)* Short form of Jebediah.

JECHONIAH *(Hebrew)* Jehovah establishes.

JEDIDIAH *(Hebrew)* Beloved of God. VARIATIONS: Jed, Jedd, Jedediah, Jedidia, Yedidia, Yedidiah, Yedidya.

JEHORAM *(Hebrew)* Jehovah is high. NOTABLES: Biblical son of Jehoshaphat, King of Judah, who succeeded his father to the throne (1 Kings 22:50). VARIATIONS: Joram.

JEHOSHAPHAT *(Hebrew)* King of Judah.

JEREMIAH *(Hebrew)* God will uplift. NOTABLES: Old Testament prophet who lived during the reign of Josiah, King of Judah (Jeremiah 1:1–3).

God Speaks to the People of Judah through Jeremiah

By his own admission, Jeremiah wasn't much of a "people person." So he felt intimidated by the responsibility God wanted to give him. The Lord told him one day that he had been chosen even before his birth for a special job. God assured Jeremiah that he would become a great prophet if he simply went where God instructed him to go and said what God told him to say. If Jeremiah followed God's lead, God would always protect him. The Lord then touched Jeremiah's lips and said he would be sending Jeremiah forth to pull down nations and overthrow kingdoms but also to plant and rebuild.

The Lord showed him prophetic scenes. "What do you see,?" the Lord asked him. Jeremiah replied, "I see a rod of an almond tree" (Jeremiah 1:11). The Lord explained that the blooming almond was a sign for Jeremiah to know that he would always have divine protection. Jeremiah said he also saw a pot boiling on a fire and pointing north (Jeremiah 1:13). God said it was the disaster he was about to pour upon the lands of the north known as Judah because of the transgressions of the people. God told Jeremiah that he must go but he would be protected. Jeremiah went into the lands of the north and told the people of Judah a story. He said that the Lord had told him to buy a linen girdle, and tie it around his waist. He was not to get it soiled or wet. After a few days, he was to take the girdle to the Euphrates and hide it in a crack of a rock. After a few weeks, he was to retrieve it. He did those things and discovered that the belt was damaged and useless. He said that God likened that belt to his people who hid themselves from Him, became marred or wicked, trusting in falsehoods, and useless like the girdle. Then Jeremiah implored the people to abandon evil and seek God.

Jeremiah heard the word of God telling him to try again to convince the people to turn away from their wickedness. He called out to the people and said that God had told him the valley of Hinnom would be the valley of slaughter unless they repented. Jeremiah threw down a clay jar and declared that just as the jar had shattered so badly that it could not be repaired so, too, would God break the people of Judah and smash their cities.

Still, Jeremiah's words fell on deaf ears. The Judeans beat and imprisoned him. After some time, they released him. And again, Jeremiah called for repentance. It was his last call. Jeremiah's prophecy was fulfilled. The Babylonians lay siege to Judah, sacking cities and taking Israelite prisoners into Babylonian captivity.

JEREMY *(Hebrew)* The Lord exalts. VARIATIONS: Jem, Jemmie, Jemmy, Jeramee, Jeramey, Jeramie, Jere,

Jereme, Jeremey, Jeremi, Jeremia, Jeremias, Jeremie, Jerimiah, Jeromy, Jerr, Jerrie, Jerry.

JERIAH *(Hebrew)* God sees; whom Jehovah regards.

JERICHO *(Arabic)* City of the moon.

JEROHAM *(Hebrew)* Whom God loves.

JESSE *(Hebrew)* God exists; gift. VARIATIONS: Jesiah, Jess, Jessey, Jessie, Jessy.

JESUS *(English form of the Hebrew word Yeoshua, Aramaic, Yeshua)* The Lord is my salvation. NOTABLES: Son of Mary whose stepfather was Joseph. Jesus is the primary figure in Christianity. VARIATIONS: Eashoa, Iesous, Yeshua.

The Temptation of Christ by Satan: A Story of Jesus

When Jesus was ready to begin his ministry he was about thirty years old. He sought out John, who was baptizing people in the Jordan River, and asked John to baptize him also.

John had baptized many people after he came out of the wilderness. He had preached that "There cometh one mightier than I after me, the latchet of whose shoes I am not worthy to stoop down and unloose" (Mark 1:7). John had told his followers that he baptized them with water but the one to come after him would baptize them with the Holy Ghost (Mark 1:8).

Jesus stood in the Jordan River near John and was baptized. A light shone upon him from heaven. The

Holy Spirit descended in the form of a dove. The voice of God boomed, "Thou art my beloved Son, in whom I am well pleased" (Mark 1:11).

After Jesus was baptized, the Holy Spirit led him into the wilderness to pray, fast, and meditate. There, Jesus lived among the wild animals and endured the extremes of nature. He remained in the desert for forty days. Near the end of that period, he had grown weak and very hungry. Satan, suspecting that Jesus had reached his weakest point, wanted to test Jesus' faith that God would protect him.

Turn that stone into bread, he told Jesus, and end your fast. But Jesus told him that people cannot live on bread alone but by every word that proceeds out of the mouth of God (Matthew 4:3–4). Then Satan took Jesus to the highest tower of the temple in Jerusalem and told him to jump off because God would send angels to catch him. Jesus told the devil, "Thou shalt not tempt the Lord thy god" (Matthew 4:7). Finally, Satan took Jesus to a towering mountain peak and showed him all the kingdoms of the world and all the beautiful things in those kingdoms. He offered them to Jesus if Jesus would worship him. Jesus ordered Satan to leave him. "Get thee hence, Satan: for it is written, Thou shalt worship the Lord thy God, and him only shalt thou serve" (Matthew 4:10).

Having failed to tempt Jesus three times, the devil left. From the heavens, angels came and ministered to Jesus. He had withstood the temptations of Satan and remained pure, triumphant, and perfect in his faith.

JETHRO *(Hebrew)* Form of Ithra; excellence. NOTA-BLES: Moses' father-in-law.

JEZER *(Hebrew)* Anything made.

JEZREEL *(Hebrew)* God will scatter; God will sow. NOTABLES: The name of a city located at the end of the Jezreel Valley during Biblical times (1 Kings 21:1–16).

JOAB *(Hebrew)* Praise the Lord. NOTABLES: Biblical son of Zeruiah who helped King David see the correctness of bringing Absalom (the king's estranged son) home (2 Samuel 14:1–3). He was the commander of King David's army but was executed when Solomon became king. VARIATIONS: Jobe.

JOACHIM *(Hebrew)* God will determine. VARIATIONS: Joaquim, Joaquin.

JOAH *(Hebrew)* God is his brother.

JOASH *(Hebrew)* The Lord has given.

JOB *(Hebrew)* Oppressed. NOTABLES: Arguably, the most afflicted man in the Old Testament. His faith in God never wavered despite incredible suffering and hardship. He lived 140 years and witnessed four generations of his descendants (Job 42:16). VARIATIONS: Joab, Jobe, Joby.

The Suffering of Job

Job, God's faithful and dutiful servant, was blessed with wealth, a wife, ten children, and thousands of sheep, camels, donkeys, and oxen.

One day, Satan, who had once been an angel in heaven but was banished to wander the earth, presented himself before God as part of the heavenly host. God asked him where he had come from. Satan told him that he had been from east to west across the earth doing evil deeds. God inquired of Satan whether or not he had seen Job, his righteous and loyal servant. Satan saw a chance to prove that Job was not as God saw him—he told God to take away all Job's good fortune and see how Job would curse the Lord.

God told Satan that he was wrong about Job. He would put Job's fate in Satan's hands as long as he did not harm Job.

Job's troubles began soon thereafter. A servant ran to him wailing that a group of raiders had taken away all the oxen and donkeys and had killed all the servants guarding them. He was the only one who managed to escape.

While Job listened to his servant, another man ran up to say that the Chaldeans stole all Job's camels and sheep and had killed the servants guarding them. Only he had escaped.

Job did not have time to digest the news from the second servant before a third man approached to tell him that all his sons and daughters were dead. They had been dining at the eldest brother's house when a powerful wind blew from across the desert, causing the house to crash down upon them. He was the only survivor.

Job tore his clothes, shaved his head, and cried out in anguish. But even with all his wealth gone and his children dead, Job still loved God and continued to praise him.

God pointed out to Satan that Job had remained righteous and loyal. Satan told God that as long as Job was healthy, he would never reject God. Take away his health and he would curse God instead. God agreed that Satan he could make Job ill, but not kill him.

While Job yet mourned the loss of his children and servants, he became ill. Boils erupted on his body, soon covering him with sores. His wife told him to forget dignity, curse God, and die. Job told her that it was not right to be loyal to God only when things were going well.

Three of Job's friends came by, Eliphas, Bildad, and Zophar from the land of Uz. Word had come to them about Job's troubles, and they wanted to be with him and offer comfort.

Sitting on the ground under the tree cleaning his skin, Job must have looked terrible. His friends wept. For seven days and nights, the four friends sat in silence. On the eighth day, Job rose to his feet and cursed the day he was born. He asked God to let him die. His friends told him that God had turned away from Job and that Job should not curse himself but rather God.

Suddenly dark clouds gathered. A storm approached and hovered over the group of men. God's voice spoke, telling them that they were doing Job a disservice by saying such things. God told them to leave; Job would pray for them, and he would hear Job's prayer. Job prayed and God heard him praying. The Lord blessed Job as never before (Job 42: 12). He acquired more animals and ten more children, and lived to be a hundred and forty years.

JOE *(Hebrew)* Short form of Joseph. VARIATIONS: Jo, Joey.

JOEL *(Hebrew)* God is Lord.

JOHANN *(German)* Form of John.

JOHN *(Hebrew)* Disciple of Jesus. NOTABLES: John the Baptist, John the Evangelist, Pope John Paul. VARIATIONS: Johann, Johannes, Jon.

John the Baptist, Forerunner of the Savior

John was born to an elderly, childless couple—Zachariah, a priest, and Elizabeth, cousin of Mary, the mother of Jesus. The angel Gabriel announced the news to Zachariah that his wife would have a son and they would name him John. The angel also appeared before Mary, when her cousin Elizabeth was six months pregnant, and announced that a son would be born of her through the Holy Spirit. She was to call him Jesus. Both births were miracles. John was to pave the way for the coming Messiah.

John grew strong in body, in mind, and in spirit. He went to live in the desert, where he dressed in animal skins and lived on locusts and honey. In the desert, he communed with the Lord. He preached the need for repentance from sin. Some believed him to be a great prophet, perhaps even the long-awaited Jewish Messiah. Many followed him. John baptized them in the Jordan River after they had confessed their sins to him.

People would ask him who he was and whether he was the Savior. John would always tell them that he had come to prepare the way for the Savior and that he was just the forerunner of Christ. Indeed, the time came when Jesus appeared with others gathered at the Jordan seeking baptism. John baptized everyone and then baptized Jesus. The heavens opened and "the

Holy Ghost descended in a bodily shape like a dove upon him, and a voice came from heaven, which said, "Thou art my beloved Son; in thee I am well pleased" (Luke 3:22).

John had been fiercely critical of the Roman ruler Herod Antipas, who had married his brother's wife, Herodias. Everyone knew that Herod Antipas was the son of King Herod who had sought to kill the infant Jesus. Herod Antipas needed to quiet John's rhetoric but he didn't want the man murdered. He simply arrested John and locked him away.

Herod's wife hated John more than her husband did. She wanted to kill John because he spoke out so publicly about her incestuous marriage. Herod knew that John had a lot of followers and that it would be a bad idea to kill John, as he was considered a wise and holy man and was well liked. Herod even went to the dungeon to visit John. He enjoyed talking with the Baptizer even though sometimes things John said confused him.

One day, Herodias devised a plan to do away with John. She knew her husband's birthday was coming and that he was planning a great banquet for his military advisors and commanders as well as certain high-ranking officials and Galilean elders. Herodias arranged for her beautiful daughter Salome to dance for everyone. Herod was delighted that Salome's dance was so well received. He told her to ask for whatever she wanted and he would give it to her, up to half of his kingdom. Salome, unsure of what to request, asked her mother what she should say.

Herodias told Salome to ask for the head of John the Baptist on a platter. That is exactly what Salome requested. Herod was angry, but he had made a promise in front of everyone and he had to honor it. He sent word to have the executioner do what must be done and bring the head of John on a platter. When the platter was brought before him, Herod gave it to Salome and she, in turn, handed it to her mother.

The followers of John learned of his death. They claimed his body and entombed it. They sent a messenger to tell Jesus. Jesus was saddened by the news and went off to be alone and mourn for John.

JOHNNY Form of John. VARIATIONS: Johnnie, Jonny.

JOHNSON *(English)* Son of John. VARIATIONS: Johnston, Jonson.

JONAH *(Hebrew)* Dove; Biblical book. NOTABLES: Old Testament prophet, son of Amittai (2 Kings 14: 25), whom was swallowed by a great fish that Jesus references in Matthew's gospel (Matthew 12:39). VARIATIONS: Jonas, Yonah, Yonas, Yunus.

Jonah Delivers a Warning to Ninevah

Jonah was a prophet of the Lord. God often commanded him to go and give the word of the Lord to people, and Jonah always followed the Lord's instruction. One day God told Jonah to go to Ninevah and tell the inhabitants of that city that God was unhappy with their wicked ways and would destroy their city if they did not repent. Because Jonah did not like Ninevah, he did not care whether or not it was spared destruction. He knew that if he delivered the Lord's warning the people would change their ways and

Ninevah would be spared. Jonah struggled to make a choice: Should he do the work the Lord required of him or run away to some other place?

He decided to flee to Joppa. There, he boarded a cargo ship headed for Tarnish. But the Lord caused a mighty wind to rise upon the waters, lifting the sea into gigantic waves that tossed the little boat. The sailors threw cargo overboard to try to keep their vessel afloat. They prayed to their various gods in many languages, but to no avail. Divine wrath seemed manifested in the churning water. The captain and his sailors found Jonah asleep. How could he sleep while they faced such peril? Get up, they ordered him, and pray to your god.

The men on board knew the storm was like no other they had ever experienced. They demanded to know who was responsible, but no one spoke. They decided to draw straws with the shortest straw indicating the person responsible for the violent storm. Jonah drew the short straw. Jonah told them that he was a Hebrew and that he worshipped God who created the heaven, earth, and seas. He confessed that he was running away from something that God had wanted him to do. The sailors asked Jonah how to make the storm subside. Jonah told them to throw him into the sea. They had no intention of murdering anyone. Instead, they just tried rowing the boat more vigorously. But the wind blew harder. The sea grew wilder. The boat tossed high and low and moved ever further from the land. Finally the captain cried out to God, pleading for the Lord not to judge them for what they were about to do. Then he and his men threw Jonah overboard. The sailors watched in wonder as the wind died down, the sea grew calm, and the sun broke through the clouds. The sailors and their captain dropped to their knees in thanksgiving and offered praise to God. They promised to always do the Lord's bidding and keep his ways.

Jonah flailed about in the sea. A giant fish swallowed him. Once inside the fish, Jonah understood that he hadn't died but remained alive in the fish's belly. God must still have a use for him. He felt remorse. He began to pray, promising the Lord that he would do what God commanded.

He remained inside the fish for three days. Then suddenly the fish spit him out upon the seashore, a short distance from Ninevah. The Lord's voice broke the silence. He again commanded Jonah to go to Ninevah and deliver his message to the people. This time Jonah followed God's instructions. The inhabitants of Ninevah repented, just as Jonah had suspected they would, and their city was saved from destruction.

JONAS *(Greek)* Form of Jonah.

JONATHAN *(Hebrew)* God gives. VARIATIONS: Johnathan, Johnathen, Johnathon, Jon, Jonathen, Jonathon, Jonnie, Jonny, Jonothon.

JORAM *(Hebrew)* Short form of Jehoram.

JORDAN *(Hebrew)* To flow; to descend. VARIATIONS: Jorden, Jordy, Jori, Jorrin.

JOSEPH *(Hebrew)* God will increase. NOTABLES: Son of Jacob and his wife Rachel. Joseph became the leader of one of the twelve tribes of Israel. VARIATIONS: Jodi, Jodie, Jody, Jose, Josecito, Josef, Joselito, Josephe, Josephus, Josip.

Joseph Is Born to Rachel and Jacob

When Jacob married Rachel's sister Leah, their union immediately produced a child. Soon Jacob and Leah had several boys, but Rachel, whom Jacob also married and loved more than her sister, had no babies. Rachel was miserable. How could her husband produce so many sons through her sister but none through her?

One day Rachel went to her husband and said, "Give me children or I die." Her demand brought a rebuke from her husband, "Am I God's stead, who hath withheld from thee the fruit of thy womb?" (Genesis 30:1–2).

Rachel believed that she had somehow incurred the displeasure of God, for he had closed her womb. So Rachel took her maid Bilhah into Jacob so that she could have a son through Bilhah. Indeed, the maidservant conceived and bore Jacob a son. They called him Dan. Then Bilhah conceived again. The second son was named Naphtali. Eventually, God heard the prayers of Rachel and "opened her womb" (Genesis 30:22). She told Jacob that God had taken away her reproach. Rachel had a son named Joseph and her sadness left her.

JOSH *(English)* Form of Joshua.

JOSHUA *(Hebrew)* Jehovah is my salvation; Jehovah saves. **NOTABLES:** Moses' successor, whom God ordered to continue leading the Jews into the land of Canaan after the death of Moses (Joshua 1:1–9). **VARIATIONS:** Jehoshua, Josh, Joshua, Yeshua.

Joshua Finishes the Exodus that Moses Began

Joshua was the son of Nun, faithful servant of Moses. Moses had sent Joshua and eleven other men, together representing the twelve tribes of Israel, to the land of Canaan to gather information about the Canaanites. Out of all the men sent, Joshua and Caleb were the only ones who believed that God actually would give the Hebrews the Promised Land. The Canaanites displayed what would prove to be fierce opposition to Jewish settlement of their territory. But because of their belief, Joshua and Caleb were allowed by God to enter the Promised Land.

God made Joshua the leader of the Hebrew people when Moses died. Sadly, neither Moses nor his brother Aaron nor sister Miriam lived to enter the Promised Land. When Joshua assumed the task of leading the Jews, the children of the Lord had not yet crossed the Jordan River. The Lord told Joshua to continue over the Jordan into the land he had promised them. He explained to Joshua that no man would ever be able to stand against "thee all the days of thy life: as I was with Moses, so I will be with thee: I will not fail thee, nor forsake thee. Be strong and of a good courage: for unto this people shalt thou divide for an inheritance the land, which I swore unto their fathers to give them" (Joshua 1:5–6).

Joshua sent two men from Shittim into Jericho to spy. The King of Jericho somehow found out about the two men, and the king sent messengers to the house of Rahab, a local harlot, to find out if the men were with her. She had hidden Joshua's men, and when the king's messengers appeared at her house she told them that the men had come and gone through the gate, but if the king's messengers hurried, they might catch up with them. When night fell, Rahab went to the men and told them of the fear that her people had of the Jews. She begged the men to give her a favor in return for what she had done—to spare the lives of her father, mother, sisters, and brothers when they return to seize the land. And the men said, "Our life for yours, if ye utter not this our business. And it shall be, when the Lord hath given us the land, that we will deal kindly and truly with thee" (Joshua 2:14). They returned to Joshua and told him that the Lord had surely delivered the land into the hands of the Hebrews because the inhabitants of that place already feared them.

Joshua and the children of the Lord rested three days. Then the priests took the Ark of the Covenant to the edge of the Jordan River. Joshua proclaimed to all assembled that they would know that the living God was before them because when the soles of the priests' feet touched the water, the water would part, allowing them to move across. And just as Joshua had foretold, "the priests that bare the ark of the covenant of the Lord stood firm on dry ground in the midst of Jordan, and all the Israelites passed over on dry ground, until all the people were passed clean over Jordan" (Joshua 3:17).

JOSIAH *(Hebrew)* God supports. VARIATIONS: Josia, Josias, Josua.

JUDAH *(Hebrew)* Praised. NOTABLES: Son of Jacob and his wife Leah and one of the leaders of the twelve tribes of Israel.

JUDAS *(Hebrew)* Form of Judah. NOTABLES: One of the disciples of Jesus was Judas, son of James, also known as Thaddeus; Jesus also had a disciple named Judas Iscariot, who betrayed him (Matthew 10:4).

Judas and His Replacement

Judas Iscariot, one of Jesus' disciples, was the treasurer for the disciples of Jesus and his followers. Judas complained about Mary using an expensive ointment to anoint Jesus' feet at Bethany when the ointment could have been sold for 300 pence and given to the poor. It was Judas who betrayed Jesus for a purse containing thirty pieces of silver, delivering him into the hands of the chief priests and setting into motion events that culminated in Jesus' death.

The surname of Judas was Iscariot. Some scholars have associated that name with the Hebrew meaning "man of Kerioth." Kerioth, according to Joshua 15:21–25, was a town in Judah. Little is known about the family life of Judas or how he came to be called to work in Jesus' ministry. The New Testament gospels of Matthew, Mark, and Luke all mention his name in conjunction with the disciple who betrayed him (Matthew 10:4; Mark 3:19; Luke 6:16). The Gospel of John also points to Judas in conjunction with the forthcoming betrayal: "Then saith one of his disciples, Judas Iscariot, Simon's son," "which should betray him?" (John 12:4).

Judas, the Bible text reveals, may have been devoted to Jesus. Jesus knew the identity of the one who would betray him, for at the Last Supper he dipped his bread and passed it to Judas. Upon this act, the devil then entered into the heart of Judas. "And after the sop Satan entered into him. Then said Jesus unto him, "That thou doest, do quickly." Now no man at the table knew for what intent he spake this unto him. For some of them thought, because Judas had the bag, that Jesus had said unto him, "Buy those things that we have need of against the feast"; or, "that he should give something to the poor" (John 13:27–29).

After the death of Judas Iscariot, who hanged himself in remorse and shame, the disciples had to choose a new member for their group. One of two men, Barsabbas and Matthias, were to be chosen. The disciples, now called Apostles, prayed for God to inspire them to make the right choice. They cast lots, and Matthias became the twelfth disciple, replacing Judas.

JUDD *(Hebrew)* Form of Judah.

JUDE *(Hebrew)* Praise God. NOTABLES: Saint Jude, patron saint of lost causes. VARIATIONS: Juda, Judah, Judas, Judd, Judson.

JUSTICE *(Latin)* Just. VARIATIONS: Justis.

K

KANIEL *(Hebrew)* Reed. VARIATIONS: Kan, Kani, Kanny.

KAYAM *(Hebrew)* Stable.

KEDEM *(Hebrew)* Old; eastern; what is in front of one. The Lord's way of describing the land to Abraham as quarters of the world, that is: "northward,

and southward, and eastward, and westward"
(Genesis 13:14).

KEFIR *(Hebrew)* Lion cub.

KEMUEL *(Hebrew)* To help God. NOTABLES: One of
the children that Milcah bore to Nahor, Abraham's
brother (Genesis 22:20–23).

KENAN *(Hebrew)* To attain. VARIATIONS: Cainan.

KITTIM *(Hebrew)* Biblical name for Cyprus. VARIATIONS: Chittim.

KOHATH *(Hebrew)* Assembly. NOTABLES: One of the
Biblical sons of Levi (Genesis 46:11).

KORAH *(Hebrew)* Bald.

KOREN *(Hebrew)* Shining. VARIATIONS: Corin, Korin.

KORESH *(Hebrew)* To dig. VARIATIONS: Choreish,
Choresh.

L

LAADAN *(Hebrew)* To put in order. NOTABLES: Biblical son of Ephraim (1 Chronicles 7:22–26). VARIATIONS: Ladan.

LABAN *(Hebrew)* White. NOTABLES: Rebekah's
brother (Jacob's uncle). Jacob fled to Laban's house
after tricking his brother Esau out of his birthright.
Jacob married Laban's daughters Leah and Rachel
(Genesis 27:43–45, 29:21–28). VARIATIONS: Leban.

LAEL *(Hebrew)* Belongs to God.

LAVI *(Hebrew)* Lion.

LAZARUS *(Greek)* Greek form of Eleazar; God's help. NOTABLES: The man whom Jesus raised from the dead (John 12:17). VARIATIONS: Eleazer, Laza, Lazare, Lazaro, Lazzro.

The Raising of Lazarus

Lazarus and his sisters Mary and Martha were Jesus' friends and followers. The family lived in a small house in Bethany, a village outside of Jerusalem. One day, a messenger, sent by the sisters of Lazarus, went to Jesus with a message that Lazarus, the friend that Jesus loved, was gravely ill. Jesus told the messenger that Lazarus's sickness would not kill him. Jesus' disciples reminded him that the Judean Jews had recently wanted to stone him to death. Jesus was not concerned about that. He knew that the illness that Lazarus suffered had taken hold of his friend for a divine purpose. Jesus would soon demonstrate the power of God.

He remained two days in Jerusalem. Suddenly, he announced to his companions that it was time to go to Judea because Lazarus had fallen asleep and must be awakened. His companions pointed out that sleep is a good thing for a sick person. They had not understood the severity of Lazarus's illness, so Jesus told them plainly, "Lazarus is dead" (John 11:14).

Two days later, Jesus arrived in Bethany. For four long days, Lazarus had lain in the tomb. Many people had gathered to pay their respects and to comfort Mary and Martha. When Martha learned that Jesus was approaching their town, she ran to meet him. She told him, "Lord, if thou hadst been here, my brother had not died. But I know, that even now, whatsoever thou wilt ask of God, God will give it thee" (John 11:21). Jesus assured her that Lazarus would rise again.

Jesus told her, "I am the resurrection, and the life: he that believeth in me, though he were dead, yet shall he live: and whosoever liveth and believeth in me shall never die" (John 11:25–26). He asked Martha if she believed him, and she said she knew he was Christ, the Son of God. Martha ran to Mary and told her that their master had come and was calling for her. Mary got up and walked out of the house. Friends and relatives went with her, thinking that she was going down to the tomb.

Mary fell at Jesus' feet, telling him that if only he would have come sooner, their beloved brother would not have died. Her suffering saddened Jesus and he wept. He asked where they had laid him. Mary offered to take him to the cave.

A large stone covered the mouth of the cave. Martha reminded Jesus that Lazarus's body had been in there for four days and by then must stink. Jesus replied that if she would believe, then she would see the glory of God. He ordered the stone rolled away. As the crowd of family and friends watched, the cave was opened. Jesus praised God and gave thanks. He cried out in a loud voice, "Lazarus, come forth" (John 11:43).

Lazarus, with the burial cloth still wrapped around his face and wearing his graveclothes, stepped out of the tomb. Jesus told those gathered to unwrap the cloth that bound Lazarus and let him go.

The crowd became animated and talked openly about the miracle. The news quickly reached Jerusalem where the Jewish elders and the Pharisees called a meeting of the Sanhedrin (council of elders) to discuss what to do about Jesus. The elders were not only priests but also court judges and leaders of the Jews. The meeting of the Sanhedrin was necessary because they believed that when word of Jesus' miracles reached the Romans, who governed the land, the Romans would take all power away from the Jewish people and oppress their nation. The council members led by Caiaphas, the Sanhedrin's high priest, discussed the coming Passover. Jesus would surely return to Jerusalem, as did many Jews who wished to purify themselves and to prepare for the Passover meal. The elders decided to issue a command that if any man knew where Jesus was, he should inform the Sanhedrin so that Jesus might be arrested. The Jewish high priest Caiaphas told them that it would be expedient that Jesus should die for the Jewish nation. And so the proposal to put Jesus to death was agreed upon.

LEBEN *(Hebrew)* Life.

LEHABIM *(Hebrew)* For understanding; instructing. NOTABLES: Biblical son of Mizraim, one of the descendants of Noah (Genesis 10:13).

LEIBEL *(Hebrew)* My lion. VARIATIONS: Leib.

LEMUEL *(Hebrew)* Devoted to God.

LEV *(Hebrew)* Heart.

LEVI *(Hebrew)* Joined to the Lord; associate. NOTABLES: The third son born to Leah and Jacob and leader of one of the twelve tribes of Israel (Genesis 29:34).

LIOR *(Hebrew)* Light. VARIATIONS: Leor.

LIRON *(Hebrew)* My song. VARIATIONS: Lyron.

LO-AMMI *(Hebrew)* Not my people. NOTABLES: Son of Hosea and Gomer (Hosea 1:8–9). VARIATIONS: Loammi.

LOT *(Hebrew)* Concealed. NOTABLES: Nephew of the Hebrew patriarch Abraham, who settled near the wicked town of Sodom and whose wife was turned into a pillar of salt (Genesis 11:27).

Lot's Wife Becomes a Pillar of Salt

Lot and his wife lived very near Sodom, a town filled with wicked men. One evening, two angels of the Lord appeared. Lot was seated at the gate of the town enjoying the evening air when he saw the angels approach. They seemed like strangers passing through, and he rose to meet them. Lot offered them lodging since night was nearly upon them. The angels told Lot that they would just stay in the street all night. But Lot pressed them and eventually they agreed to be his guests.

The Sodomite men had seen the angels come to town and wanted to meet Lot's guests. The Sodomites went to Lot's house and called for Lot to bring out the men so that they could have intimate relations with them. Lot went out of his house and closed the door behind him, leaving his guests safely inside. He begged the men of Sodom not to be so wicked. He even offered his own daughters, but the Sodomites became enraged and adamant. Lot refused the mob entrance into his home and did not comply with their request to turn over his guests. The angels made the Sodomites go blind.

In the morning, the angels told Lot to take his wife and members of his family and flee because the Lord would destroy the twin cities of Sodom and Gomorrah. The angels further instructed Lot that no one should look back.

Perhaps because Sodom was the home of his wife or because Lot liked the land he had prospered on, he begged the angels of the Lord to spare the city. But the fate of the cities was already sealed. The angels of the Lord escorted Lot and his wife and daughters away from Sodom. Soon fire and brimstone fell upon those cities and all of the plain, destroying everything. Lot's wife, perhaps to steal just one last nostalgic look at her town, turned back for a final look. Instantly, she became a pillar of salt (Genesis 19:26).

LUD *(Hebrew)* Strife.

LUDIM *(Hebrew)* Generation; nativity.

LUKE *(English)* Form of Lucas. NOTABLES: Physician friend of the Apostle Paul; perhaps source for the canonical Gospel of Luke. VARIATIONS: Luc.

M

MACCABEE *(Hebrew)* Hammer. VARIATIONS: Macabee, Makabi.

MACHPELAH *(Hebrew)* Double.

MADAI *(Hebrew)* Judging; garment.

MAGOG *(Hebrew)* Covering; roof; dissolving.

MALACHI *(Hebrew)* Messenger. VARIATIONS: Malachai, Malachie, Malachy, Malechy.

MALIK *(Arabic)* Master.

MALKI *(Hebrew)* My king.

MANASSEH *(Hebrew)* One who causes to forget. NOTABLES: Son of Hephzibah and Hezekiah who became ruler of Judah upon his father's death (2 Kings 20:21).

The Children of Israel Move Further Away from God

Manasseh was twelve when his father Hezekiah died. Hezekiah's legacy of building a strong Hebrew nation that emphasized devotion to God and obeisance to the Lord's laws was reversed under the leadership of Manasseh. The young king began constructing pagan temples. He abused his power as king and was seen by the people as ruthless and cruel. During his rule, the Israelites turned away from God more and more.

Although the Lord spoke to Manasseh and the Israelites, they did not listen. Then the Assyrian army arrived and took Manasseh in brass chains to Babylon. Only in a place of deep, dark fear did Manasseh finally turn back to God, praying for help. God heard and responded. Manasseh was finally allowed to return to Jerusalem. There, he set about ridding the land of strange gods. He destroyed altars erected for pagan worship. He told the people of Judah to worship and serve the Lord as he had begun to do. He set up new altars to God and offered gifts of peace and thanks upon them. In this way, Manasseh turned back on his previous life of sin and remained faithful to the Lord of Abraham until he died. His reign lasted fifty-five years.

MANUEL *(Hebrew)* Form of Emmanuel.

MAOZ *(Hebrew)* Strength.

MARCUS *(Latin)* Warlike. VARIATIONS: Marco, Marcos.

MARK *(English)* Form of Marcus. NOTABLES: The surname of a young Christian man to whose home the Apostle Peter went after leaving prison (Acts 12:12).

MARTIN *(Latin)* Warlike. NOTABLES: religious leader Martin Luther, Dr. Martin Luther King Jr. VARIATIONS: Mart, Martan, Martel, Marten, Martey, Martie, Martinas, Martiniano, Martinka, Martino, Martinos, Martins, Marto, Marton, Marty, Martyn, Mertin.

MARTY *(English)* Short form of Martin.

MATANIAH *(Hebrew)* Gift from God. VARIATIONS: Matania, Matanya, Matitia, Matitiah, Matityah, Matityahu, Mattaniah, Mattathias, Matya.

MATTAN *(Hebrew)* Gift; slender. NOTABLES: Priest of Baal, murdered when Jehoiada attacked Queen Athaliah when she tried to usurp the throne from its rightful heir, her grandson Joash (2 Kings 11:18; 2 Chronicles 23:17).

MATTHEW *(Hebrew)* God's gift. NOTABLES: Disciple of Jesus for whom one of the New Testament gospel accounts is named. Jesus' Sermon on the Mount is found in the Gospel of Matthew. VARIATIONS: Mateo, Mateus, Mathe, Mathew, Mathia, Mathias, Mathieu, Matias, Matt, Matteo, Matthaus, Matthia, Matthias, Mattias, Matty.

Jesus' Sermon on the Mount: A Story of Matthew

Jesus' ministry lasted only three years, but during that short time he changed the thinking of many in ancient Palestine. Jesus embedded his gems of wisdom in parables, sayings, and stories. He not only shared his beliefs with multitudes of people, he healed the sick and lame, gave sight to the blind, exorcised evil spirits, and raised the dead. His celebrity soon extended far beyond Galilee. Crowds followed him everywhere he went. People desperate to hear positive messages in their lives flocked to hear his words of wisdom.

One day, while he walked along the shore of the Sea of Galilee, he observed the crowd following him increasing in number. So Jesus and his disciples walked up the mountain. When he could see everyone, Jesus addressed those assembled.

"Blessed are the poor in spirit," he began, "for theirs is the kingdom of heaven. Blessed are they that mourn: for they shall be comforted. Blessed are the meek: for they shall inherit the earth. Blessed are they who hunger and thirst after righteousness: for they shall be filled.

Blessed are the merciful: for they shall obtain mercy. Blessed are the pure in heart: for they shall see God. Blessed are the peacemakers: for they shall be called the children of God. Blessed are they who are persecuted for righteousness' sake: for theirs is the kingdom of heaven. Blessed are ye, when men shall revile you, and persecute you, and shall say all manner of evil against you falsely, for my sake." (Matthew 5:3–11)

He told everyone before him that day to not think that he had come to abolish the Law of the Jews or the Prophets, for he had come not to abolish but rather to fulfill their prophecy. In the years following his death, his words continued to survive in the gospel messages that the disciples shared with one another and with the people of many lands.

Jesus told the Jews and others assembled that day that he had not come to destroy the Law but to fulfill it (Matthew 5:17). He said, "For verily I say unto you, till heaven and earth pass, one jot or one title shall in no wise pass from the law, till all be fulfilled" (Matthew 5:18). He explained that those who broke the commandments would be called the smallest and whoever preached the commandments he proposed would be called great in the kingdom of heaven (Matthew 5:19).

Do not commit murder, he told them, or think violent thoughts. He said that they may have been taught to take revenge, an eye for an eye, but he said resist evil. If someone hurts you, turn the other cheek. He gave them a new axiom to live by, telling everyone to love their enemies, pray for those who would harm them, and love their neighbors as they loved themselves.

Jesus admonished his listeners not to make a public display of their faith or their giving of charitable gifts. Those who believe and give have already received their rewards. Close the door to your room and pray in private, he told them, and pray to the unseen Father; and he gave them a prayer to offer the Lord. "Our Father which art in heaven, Hallowed by thy name. Thy kingdom come, Thy will be done in earth, as it is in heaven. Give us this day our daily bread. And forgive us our debts, as we forgive our debtors. And lead us not into temptation, but deliver us from evil: For thine is the kingdom, and the power, and the glory, for ever. Amen" (Matthew 6:9–13).

Forgive the one who sins against you and God will forgive your sins, Jesus told them. Do not judge other people, or you will be judged. Do not spend your life seeking only wealth because it is does not last. Put your efforts into gaining treasures in heaven. Do not criticize the failings of others but examine your own. Pray to your Father for what you need. Ask and you will receive; seek and you will find; knock and the door will be opened to you. These are only a few of the many teachings in the sermon Jesus offered that day. His greatest commandment was to love one another. He also said that the person who had heard his words and put them into practice would be like the man who built his house upon a rock. Storms and floods could still come, but with such a strong foundation, the house would not be harmed.

Jesus' discourse on the mountain that day became known as the Sermon on the Mount. His message was so powerful that people regarded him with high esteem. He was no ordinary teacher of the Law. Many believed that he was indeed the Jewish messiah who would be called the Prince of Peace, prophesied in the Old Testament book of Isaiah 9:6.

MATTHIAS *(Hebrew)* Gift of the Lord; derivative of Matthew. NOTABLES: The name of the disciple of Jesus who was selected by the other disciples by drawing lots to replace Judas (Acts 1:15–26).

MEIR *(Hebrew)* Bright one. VARIATIONS: Mayer, Meyer, Myer.

MELCHIOR *(Hebrew)* King.

MENACHEM *(Hebrew)* Comforting. VARIATIONS: Menahem, Mendel.

MENDEL *(Hebrew)* Wisdom. VARIATIONS: Mendeley, Mendell.

MERARI *(Hebrew)* Bitter. NOTABLES: The father of Mahli and Mushi (1 Chronicles: 24:26).

MESHACH *(Hebrew)* Artist. NOTABLES: One of three men, friends of Daniel, who refused Nebuchadnezzar's order to bow down and worship the golden idol made in his image (Daniel 1:7, 2:49, 3:12–30).

MICAH *(Hebrew)* Form of Michael.

MICHAEL *(Hebrew)* Who is like God. NOTABLES: A Benjamite man named as one of the many ancestors and descendants of King Saul (1 Chronicles 8:16). There are roughly ten other individuals in the Bible with the name of Michael. VARIATIONS: Makis, Micah, Micha, Michail, Michak, Michal, Michalek, Michau, Micheal, Michel, Michele, Mick,

Mickel, Mickey, Mickie, Micky, Miguel, Mihail, Mihailo, Mihkel, Mikaek, Mikael, Mikala, Mike, Mikelis, Mikey, Mikhail, Mikhalis, Mikhos, Mikkel, Mikko, Mischa, Misha, Mitch, Mitchel, Mitchell.

MISHAEL *(Hebrew)* Who is what God is. NOTABLES: Son of Uzziel and brother to Elzaphan and Zithri (Exodus 6:22).

MIZRAIM *(Hebrew)* Fortresses. NOTABLES: A descendant of Noah who was one of the sons of Ham along with Cush, Phut, and Canaan (Genesis 10: 6).

MORAN *(Hebrew)* Guide.

MORDECAI *(Hebrew)* Warlike. VARIATIONS: Mordche, Mordechai, Mordi, Motche.

MOSES *(Hebrew)* The son of water; one who draws out. NOTABLES: The Biblical leader who received the Ten Commandments from God and led the ancient Hebrews in their exodus from Egypt. VARIATIONS: Moise, Moises, Moisey, Mose, Mosese, Mosha, Moshe, Moss, Moyse, Moze, Mozes.

MUPPIM *(Hebrew)* Covering; from the mouth. NOTABLES: One of the sons of Benjamin (Genesis 46:21).

MUSHI *(Hebrew)* Withdrawn. NOTABLES: One of the men in the Biblical family of Levi (Exodus 6:19).

N

NAAMAN *(Hebrew)* Pleasantness. NOTABLES: A Syrian military soldier in the army of King Ben-Hadad who became cured of leprosy through the intervention of the prophet Elisha (2 Kings 5:1).

NAARAI *(Hebrew)* Youthful.

NAASHON *(Hebrew)* Enchanter. NOTABLES: Biblical brother of Elisheba, wife of Aaron (Exodus 6:23). VARIATIONS: Naason.

NABAL *(Hebrew)* Foolish.

NABOTH *(Hebrew)* Words; prophecies. NOTABLES: The owner of a vineyard who is murdered by Queen Jezebel (1 Kings 21:14).

The Taking of Naboth's Vineyard

An Israelite named Naboth owned a lush vineyard near the king's palace in the city of Jezreel. King Ahab, the monarch of the northern kingdom of Israel, had noticed the vineyard during his frequent outings and had begun to covet it. He offered Naboth compensation for the vineyard, but Naboth was adamant that his vineyard was not for sale. Generations of Naboth's family had previously owned and tended that vineyard. Beautiful and productive, the vineyard held many memories for Naboth. King Ahab, however, was used to getting what he wanted. He would wait.

Ahab was married to a conniving and powerful queen named Jezebel. She knew of his desire for the vineyard and believed she could get it for her husband. She devised a plan to have Naboth stoned to death. With Naboth dead, Ahab happily took possession of the vineyard.

But soon, word of Naboth's death reached Elijah the Tishbite, a powerful Hebrew prophet. The prophet immediately went to the king and expressed his outrage. He warned Ahab that the Lord would inflict "evil upon thee, and will take away thy posterity" (1 Kings 21:21). Elijah declared that Jezebel, who had concocted the plan in the first place, would not escape the justice of the Lord. "The dogs shall eat Jezebel by the wall of Jezreel" (1 Kings 21:23).

Ahab tore his clothes, put on sackcloth, and fasted. He lay upon the sackcloth and "went softly" (1 Kings 21:27) meaning that King Ahab's strength was gone and sorrow had taken hold of him. The monarch fell into a state of deep remorse over his wife's actions and his own desire to have Naboth's vineyard at any price. The Lord told Elijah that Ahab had humbled himself so that instead of bringing evil upon the king, the Lord would bring evil upon the sons of the king and his house (1 Kings 21:29). No divine mercy was shown Jezebel either. She died—thrown by her servants out of a palace window—and her corpse was devoured by dogs.

NACHMAN *(Hebrew)* Comfort. VARIATIONS: Nahum.

NADAB *(Hebrew)* Liberal. NOTABLES: Son born to Aaron and Elisheba (Exodus 6:23).

NAHALIEL *(Hebrew)* Valley of God.

NAHUM *(Hebrew)* Comforter.

NAMIR *(Hebrew)* Leopard.

NAPHTALI *(Hebrew)* My wrestling. NOTABLES: The son born to Jacob and his wife Rachel's maidservant

Bilhah. Naphtali became the leader of one of the twelve tribes of Israel (Genesis 30:8).

NAPHTUHIM *(Hebrew)* Meaning obscure. NOTABLES: One of the Biblical descendants of Noah (Genesis 10:13).

NATHAN *(Hebrew)* Giver. VARIATIONS: Natan, Nathen, Nathon.

NATHANIEL *(Hebrew)* Gift from God. VARIATIONS: Nathanael, Nathanial, Nathanie.

NEBUCHADNEZZAR *(Babylonian)* Tears and groans of judgment. NOTABLES: Biblical King of Babylon during the reign of Johoiakim, King of Judah (Daniel 1:1).

Nebuchadnezzar's Nightmare

King Nebuchadnezzar suffered from a nightmare that he did not understand. The king needed his sleep, for by day he had to rule over a vast empire known as Babylon. He ordered his magicians, astrologers, sorcerers, and the Chaldeans to interpret his dream, but they were unable to do so. Furious, the king decreed that all the wise men of Babylon were to be destroyed.

Word reached Daniel, prompting him to ask why the king so hastily would have issued such a decree. Nebuchadnezzar previously had established a relationship with the young captive Israelite because Daniel was wise beyond his years. The king had given Daniel a position as one of the nation's highest-level advisors and had appointed three of Daniel's friends—

Hananiah, Mishael, and Azariah—as governors of various Babylonian provinces.

Daniel knew that God revealed deep and secret things and gave wisdom to the wise. He understood that God alone knew the darkness and light to be found in each human. Daniel told Arioch, the man the king sent to destroy all the nation's wise men, to delay in the killing until he could give the correct interpretation of the dream.

Arioch accompanied Daniel into the king's chambers where Daniel told the king about his God in heaven, who could reveal secrets and make known to the king that which would come in the latter days. Then Daniel told the king what thoughts were passing through the king's mind in sleep. He explained that they were visions that God was giving the king. He went on to describe the image that was recurring in the king's nightmare.

"This great image, whose brightness was excellent, stood before thee; and the form thereof was terrible. This image's head was of fine gold, his breast and his arms of silver, his belly and his thighs of brass, his legs of iron, his feet part of iron and part of clay" (Daniel 2:31–33). Daniel went on to describe a stone that the king had cut out and had used to smash the statue into so many pieces like chaff on a summer threshing floor that wind carried away. The stone became a mountain so large that it contained the entire earth.

Daniel explained that God had given Nebuchadnezzar his power over the land and said that the head of gold was none other than the king himself. After the rule of Nebuchadnezzar would come another kingdom, inferior to that of the present kingdom.

Following that, another period would see a third kingdom of brass, and after that, a fourth kingdom would arise that would be as strong as iron. The toes, which were part iron and clay, represented a kingdom divided. The kingdom that God would set up would not break into pieces like the iron, brass, clay, silver, and gold, but would be like the mountain rising up over the whole earth and never to be destroyed.

The king was so grateful to Daniel for his insights that he fell down and worshipped Daniel. He ordered his subject to pay oblations to Daniel and that sweet incense be burned. He promoted Daniel to ruler over the whole province of Babylon and chief of all the governors and wise men of that nation. Further, he also made Daniel's companions Shadrach, Meshach, and Abednego provincial governors. But it was Daniel who thereafter "sat in the gate of the king" (Daniel 2:49).

NEDAVIAH *(Hebrew)* Charity of the Lord. VARIATIONS: Nedabiah, Nedavia, Nedavya.

NEHEMIAH *(Hebrew)* Lord's comfort. VARIATIONS: Nechemiah, Nechemya.

NER *(Hebrew)* Light. NOTABLES: Biblical man whose son was the captain of King Saul's host (1 Samuel 14:50).

NERIAH *(Hebrew)* Lamp of Jehovah.

NETANIAH *(Hebrew)* God has given. VARIATIONS: Netania, Netanya, Nethaniah.

NICHOLAS *(Greek)* Victorious. VARIATIONS: Niccolo, Nichol, Nick, Nickolas, Nickolaus, Nicol, Nicolaas,

Nicolas, Nikita, Niklas, Niklos, Niko, Nikolais, Niko-
las, Nikolaus, Nikolo, Nikolos, Nikos, Nikula.

NIMROD *(Hebrew)* Rebel.

NIRAM *(Hebrew)* Fertile meadow.

NISAN *(Hebrew)* Miracle. VARIATIONS: Nissan.

NOADIAH *(Hebrew)* Meeting with God. NOTABLES:
The Levite son of Bennui who (with Meremoth,
son of Uriah the priest; Eleazar, son of Phinehas;
and Jozabad, the son of Jeshua) weighed the sacred
silver and gold vessels after they had been returned
from Babylon to Jerusalem (Ezra 8:33). VARIATIONS:
Noadia, Noadya.

NOAH *(Hebrew)* Comfort *(Palestinian)* I go. NOTABLES:
Biblical builder of the Ark that survived the flood
(Genesis 6:13–14). VARIATIONS: Noach, Noak, Noe,
Noi, Noy.

Noah and the Great Deluge

Noah is perhaps the most famous of all the biblical
figures except for Jesus. He was the son of Lamech,
who lived to be one hundred and eighty-two. Noah's
grandfather Methuselah was the oldest man to have
ever lived, according to the Bible. He died at the age
of nine hundred and sixty-nine. Of course, there were
two men in the Bible who did not die at all but were
taken up to heaven—Enoch, who walked with God
and was no more (Genesis 5:22–24), and Elijah the
prophet, who was transported into heaven by a whirl-
wind (2 Kings 2:11). Noah reached the age of nine

hundred and fifty before he passed away. By the time of his death, the flood that had made him famous and had covered the world was a distant memory. It had taken place three hundred and fifty years earlier.

During ancient times, children were given names that signified something about the family, their birth order, their society, the culture in which they lived, the greater world, or their destiny, among other things. Lamech named his son Noah because he was expected to comfort humankind by surviving a great flood. The name of Noah comes from the Hebrew root *noham*, meaning "comfort."

God gave Noah a warning about the coming deluge. Because of the wickedness of humans, the earth was filled with violence. God saw the corruption of his creation but also saw the goodness and righteousness of Noah. Some sources assert that God gave humanity a 120-year period of grace to redeem itself or face a great deluge that would wipe the earth clean of its ungodliness (Genesis 6:3).

The Lord decided to destroy what he had created and to start over again with Noah and his family. Noah's wife and sons, Shem, Ham, and Japeth, and their wives and children would be the only humans spared. God told Noah how to construct a massive ark that when finished would hold Noah's family as well as two of every kind of plant and animal species to repopulate the earth.

Noah built the ark, and included an altar. Noah moved in, just as God had instructed. Within seven days the rain began. It did not stop for forty days and forty nights. The ark was lifted up and floated safely upon the water. Gradually the mountains were covered.

"And every living substance was destroyed which was upon the face of the ground, both man, and cattle, and the creeping things, and the fowl of the heaven; and they were destroyed from the earth: and Noah only remained alive, and they that were with him in the ark. And the waters prevailed upon the earth a hundred and fifty days" (Genesis 7:23–24).

A full year passed before the waters receded and the earth dried enough to expose land masses. To detect them, Noah regularly sent out birds. Noah's first act before beginning life in the new world was to prepare a burnt offering to the Lord as a sacrifice of thanksgiving (Genesis 8:20). He continued to live another three hundred and fifty years.

NOAM *(Hebrew)* Delight.

NURI *(Hebrew/Arabic)* Fire. VARIATIONS: Noori, Nury.

NURIEL *(Hebrew/Arabic)* Fire of God. VARIATIONS: Nuria, Nuriah, Nurial.

O

OBADIAH *(Hebrew)* Servant of God. VARIATIONS: Obadias, Obe, Obed, Obediah, Obie, Ovadiach, Ovadiah.

OBED *(Hebrew)* Worshipping God.

OHAD *(Hebrew)* Might.

OMEGA *(Hebrew)* Great.

ONAM *(Hebrew)* Strong.

ONESIMUS *(Greek)* Profitable. NOTABLES: Servant owned by Philemon, Christian and friend of the Apostle Paul (Philemon 1:10)

OREN *(Hebrew)* Pine tree. VARIATIONS: Orin, Orran, Orren, Orrin.

OREV *(Hebrew)* Raven.

OVED *(Hebrew)* Worshiper. VARIATIONS: Obed.

OZ *(Hebrew)* Power.

OZIAS *(Greek)* Strength from the Lord; form of Uzziah.

P

PAGIEL *(Hebrew)* Worships God.

PATRICK *(Latin)* Noble man. NOTABLES: Patron saint of Ireland Saint Patrick. VARIATIONS: Paddey, Paddy, Padraic, Padraig, Padruig, Pat, Patek, Patric, Patrice, Patricio, Patricius, Patrik, Patrizio, Patrizius, Patryk.

PAUL *(Latin)* Small. NOTABLES: Self-proclaimed Apostle who successfully spread the Christian gospel to Asia Minor and whose letters are contained in the New Testament. VARIATIONS: Pablo, Pal, Pali, Palika, Pall, Paolo, Pasha, Pashenka, Pashka, Paska, Paulin, Paulino, Paulis, Paulo, Pauls, Paulus, Pauly, Pavel, Pavils, Pavlicek, Pavlik, Pavlo, Pavlousek, Pawel, Pawl, Pol, Poul.

Saul's Conversion and Name Change to Paul

Saul made a name for himself as a persecutor of Jesus' followers. He was a Pharisee, born in Tarsus, a Jew and a also a Roman citizen. He saw the Jesus group as a splinter sect of Jews who espoused beliefs that he did not embrace, and he did not believe that Jesus was the long-awaited Messiah. For a time he was one of the greatest enemies of the followers of Jesus.

He combed the streets of Jerusalem seeking disciples and followers of Christ to have them thrown into dungeons. When they fled the holy city, Saul pursued them beyond the gates into the countryside. After receiving permission from the high priest to arrest Jesus' followers, he set off on the road to Damascus. Just before he entered the city, a blinding white flash of light struck him. Saul fell to the ground. A voice called out from the heavens. "Saul, Saul, why are you persecuting me?" Saul understood it to be the voice of God. "Who are you?" Saul asked. The voice replied, "Jesus."

Now Saul lay trembling and astonished. He asked the Lord what he wanted him to do and was told that he should go into the city and wait. A messenger would come. Saul rose to his feet. But he could not see. The men traveling with him escorted him into Damascus.

After Saul had waited for three days without food or water, a disciple of Jesus named Ananias came to the place where Saul was staying. The Lord had told Ananias in a vision that he was to go to the house of Judas and seek a man called Saul of Tarsus. And then when he had found Saul, he was to place his hands on Saul's eyes to heal the blindness.

Ananias didn't want to help the persecutor of the Christians, but God told him that Saul was his instrument. He would use Saul to carry forth his name to the Gentiles, kings, and children of Israel. So Ananias entered the house and did as God had commanded. He put his hands over Saul's eyes and said, "Brother Saul, the Lord, even Jesus, that appeared unto thee in the way as thou camest, hath sent me, that thou mightest receive thy sight, and be filled with the Holy Ghost" (Acts 9:17). Immediately, Saul's sight returned and he arose and was baptized.

Right away, he entered the synagogues and preached that Christ was the Son of God. And the Jews were confused because this same Saul previously had been persecuting the Christians. Now he had joined them. Saul increased in his spiritual power. After his conversion, he became known as Paul. He confused the Jews at Damascus more every day. After a time, they decided that he had to be killed. They gave orders to the guards at the city gates to watch for him day and night. However, some followers of Paul helped him escape through a hole in the city wall. He climbed into a basket that they lowered with ropes.

Paul hurried back to Jerusalem. Jesus' disciples were afraid of him and did not believe he was a disciple of their teacher. Barnabas alone believed Paul. He recounted Paul's story of how the Lord had come upon him while he was on the road to Damascus. He told of Paul's powerful conversion and baptism, and how since that time Paul had been preaching the name of Jesus. Finally, the Apostles accepted Paul.

Paul continued sharing the word of God with the people of Jerusalem, but soon they, too, wanted to kill him. The Apostles learned of an attempt against Paul and decided the best place for him was Tarsus in Asia Minor (modern Turkey). There, Paul could serve the Lord through work with the Christian churches around that region. Because of Paul's efforts, a great many people, Gentile and Jew, became Christians.

PEDAHEL *(Hebrew)* God redeems. VARIATIONS: Pedael.

PEDAT *(Hebrew)* Atonement.

PENUEL *(Hebrew)* God's face or in the image of God. NOTABLES: Father of Gedor (1 Chronicles 4:4).

PERACH *(Hebrew)* Flower.

PERACHIAH *(Hebrew)* God's flower. VARIATIONS: Perachia, Perachya.

PESACH *(Hebrew)* Spared; the name for Passover. VARIATIONS: Pessach.

PETER *(Greek)* Rock. NOTABLES: Simon Bar-Jonah—Simon, son of Jonah—whom Jesus renamed Cephas (Peter), meaning rock (*petra* in Latin) or stone, was the chief disciple of Christ (Matthew 16:17–18). VARIATIONS: Pearce, Pearson, Pearsson, Peat, Peder, Pedro, Peers, Peet, Peirce, Petey, Petie, Petras, Petro, Petronio, Petros, Pierce, Piero, Pierre, Pierrot, Pierrson, Piers, Pierson, Piet, Pieter, Pietro, Piotr, Pyotr.

Peter Slices a Man's Ear That Jesus Restores

In ancient times, a village known as Bethsaida stood on the northern coast of the Sea of Galilee. There, a local Galilean fisherman named Simon Bar-Jona plied the plentiful waters with his brother, Andrew. According to the Gospel of Matthew, as Jesus was walking along the seashore he spotted the brothers working the net. He called out to Simon and Andrew just as they were casting their net into the sea.

Jesus said, "Follow me, and I will make you fishers of men" (Matthew 4:18–19). Hearing those words, Simon and Andrew abandoned their work and followed Jesus. Walking with Jesus, they soon came upon two other brothers, James and John, sons of Zebedee, who were fishing that day with their father on the family boat. James and John soon joined Jesus and their friends Simon and Andrew. These two sets of brothers, all fishermen, were the first called by Jesus to become his disciples. In time there would be twelve disciples and many followers. Multitudes gathered to witness Jesus speaking in parables, healing the sick, and offering prayers to God.

Simon loved Jesus and believed that Jesus was the long-awaited messiah. He confessed his belief to Jesus, and Jesus said, "Thou art Simon the son of Jona: thou shalt be called Cephas, which is by interpretation, a stone" (John 1:42). In Latin *petra* is the word for rock or stone, so Simon soon became known as Peter or Simon Peter.

Peter loved Jesus and was loyal to him. In the gospel accounts in the Bible, he is portrayed often as the spokesperson for the disciples. But Peter was flawed, as all humans are. Peter's weakness was a mercurial temper. His outbursts often brought upon him a chastising or rebuke from Jesus. The New Testament's four gospels all mention that Jesus prophesied during the

Last Supper that Peter would deny him three times during that night before the cock crowed at dawn. It was a prophecy that proved true as events played out, culminating in the arrest and crucifixion of Jesus.

The Gospel of John notes that Peter defended Jesus from the soldiers on the night of the Savior's arrest when he cut off the ear of the servant of the High Priest. Jesus rebuked Peter for such a violent action. The Gospel of Luke doesn't say it was Peter who did the cutting but says "Suffer ye thus far. And he touched his ear, and healed him" (Luke 22:47–51).

PHANUEL *(Hebrew)* Vision of God; face of the Divine. NOTABLES: Father of Anna, the prophetess who met Jesus and his parents in the temple (Luke 2:36).

PHAREZ *(Hebrew)* Division; rupture; breach. NOTABLES: The name of Judah's son born to him by Tamar, his daughter-in-law (Genesis 38:29). VARIATIONS: Perez, Phares.

PHILEMON *(Greek)* Kiss; who kisses.

PHILIP *(Greek)* Lover of horses. NOTABLES: Disciple of Jesus. VARIATIONS: Felipe, Felipino, Fil, Filib, Filip, Filipo, Filippo, Fillipek, Fillipp, Fillips, Phil, Philippel, Phill, Phillip, Phillipe, Phillipos, Phillipp, Phillippe, Phillips, Pilib, Pippy.

PHILO *(Greek)* Loving.

PHINEAS *(Hebrew)* Oracle. VARIATIONS: Pinchas, Pincus.

PONTIUS *(Latin)* Belonging to the sea. **NOTABLES:** Pontius Pilate, the Roman prefect of Judea who ordered the death of Jesus (Matthew 27:24–26).

Pontius Pilate Condemns Jesus to Death

Although the Jews had their Sanhedrin, or council of elders, who had the power to rule and judge them, they still had to be accountable to the Roman governor. In Jerusalem, in the year of Jesus' death, that man was Pontius Pilate. It was before Pilate that Jesus was taken by the chief priests of the Sanhedrin. They told Pontius Pilate that because of all the trouble Jesus was causing, "forbidding to give tribute to Caesar, saying that he himself is Christ the King" (Luke 23:2), he had to be put to death. That could be done only upon the order of Pilate.

Pontius Pilate asked Jesus directly if he was the King of the Jews. Jesus replied, "Thou sayest it" (Luke 23:3). Pilate said to the chief priests that he found no fault in Jesus. But they were fiercely adamant that Jesus must be stopped because he was stirring up all the Jewry from Galilee to Jerusalem. When Pilate heard the word "Galilee," he asked if Jesus was a Galilean. He promptly sent Jesus to Herod's jurisdiction to let Herod handle the problem.

Pilate, however, had not seen the end of Jesus. Herod could not get Jesus to answer questions that might enable him to pronounce the death. He had hoped Jesus might perform a miracle, but that didn't happen either. The learned rabbis (who knew the Law) and the chief priests present ridiculed Jesus and accused him of various crimes and violations of the Law. This inflamed Herod's temper and he wanted to punish Jesus as much as the Jews did. He allowed his soldiers to demean and demoralize Jesus. They mockingly dressed Jesus in royal robes. In the end, however, Herod sent Jesus back to Pilate.

While Pilate pondered the situation, his wife sent a message telling him that she had had terrible dreams about the persecution of Jesus. She warned Pilate not to have anything to do with Jesus' death. During Passover, the custom was to give one prisoner his freedom and the other death. The people made the choice. Pilate knew that the Jewish high priests were unhappy with Jesus because of his popularity. The other Jewish prisoner at the time was a man named Barabbas, a murderer. Pilate opted to let the people decide which of them would live and which would be crucified.

The crowd in his courtyard was given the choice. The high priests exhorted the crowd to cry out for the crucifixion of Jesus and to let Barabbas go free. Pontius delivered Jesus to them to be put to death. "And Pilate wrote a title, and put it on the cross. And the writing was, JESUS OF NAZARETH THE KING OF THE JEWS. This title then read any of the Jews: for the place where Jesus was crucified was nigh to the city: and it was written in Hebrew, and Greek, and Latin. Then said the chief priests of the Jews to Pilate, "Write not, The King of the Jews; but that he said, I am the King of the Jews." Pilate answered, "What I have written I have written" (John 19:19–22).

PORFIRIO *(Greek)* Purple stone. VARIATIONS: Porphirios, Prophyrios.

POTIPHERAH *(Hebrew)* That scatters or demolishes. NOTABLES: The Biblical priest whose daughter Asenath was given to Joseph for a wife by Pharaoh (Genesis 41:45). VARIATIONS: Potiphar.

PROSPER *(Latin)* Fortunate. VARIATIONS: Prospero.

PUTIEL *(Hebrew)* God is my fatness.

Q

QUIRINIUS *(Latin)* Warrior. NOTABLES: Roman governor of Syria whose full name in Latin was Publius Sulpicius Quirinius of Syria and who ordered a census to be taken throughout the Roman Empire. (Luke 2:1–2). VARIATIONS: Cyrenius.

QUIRINUS *(Latin)* Form of Quirinius.

R

RABBI *(Hebrew)* My master.

RACHIM *(Hebrew)* Compassion. VARIATIONS: Racham, Rachmiel, Raham, Rahim.

RANON *(Hebrew)* Joyful song.

RAPHAEL *(Hebrew)* God has healed. VARIATIONS: Rafael, Rafel, Rafello, Raffaello.

RAZIEL *(Hebrew)* The Lord is my secret. VARIATIONS: Raz.

REHOBOAM *(Hebrew)* He who enlarges the people; who gives the people freedom. NOTABLES: Son of

King Solomon who succeeded his father (1 Kings 11:43). VARIATIONS: Roboam.

REUBEN *(Hebrew)* Behold a son. NOTABLES: First-born son of Leah and Jacob and leader of one of the twelve ancient Hebrew tribes of Israel (Genesis 29:32). VARIATIONS: Reuban, Reubin, Reuven, Reuvin, Rube, Ruben, Rubin, Rubu.

REX *(Latin)* King.

RIPHATH *(Hebrew)* Release; pardon. NOTABLES: One of the Hebrews mentioned in the genealogy of Noah's descendants born after the flood (Genesis 10:3).

RISHON *(Hebrew)* First.

ROBOAM *(Greek)* Form of Rehoboam.

RONI *(Hebrew)* Joyful.

ROSH *(Hebrew)* Head.

ROZEN *(Hebrew)* Leader.

RUBEN *(Hebrew)* Form of Reuben.

S

SADOC *(Greek)* Form of Zadok.

SAMSON *(Hebrew)* Sun. VARIATIONS: Sampson, Sanson, Sansone.

SAMUEL *(Hebrew)* God listens. VARIATIONS: Sam, Sammie, Sammy, Samouel, Samuele, Samuello.

SAUL *(Hebrew)* Asked for. NOTABLES: The man whom Samuel anointed as the king who would lead the Hebrews (1 Samuel 9:17, 10:1).

SEBASTIAN *(Latin)* One from Sebastia, an ancient Roman city. VARIATIONS: Seb, Sebastien, Sebbie.

SELAH *(Hebrew)* Song.

SERAPHIM *(Greek)* The angels *(Hebrew)* fiery. VARIATIONS: Serafin, Serafino, Seraphimus.

SERED *(Hebrew)* Fear. NOTABLES: One of Zebulun's sons (Genesis 46:14).

SERENO *(Latin)* Calm.

SETH *(Hebrew)* To appoint. NOTABLES: Son of Adam and Eve, born after their son Cain slew his brother Abel (Genesis 4:25).

SHADRACH *(Babylonian)* Under the command of Aku (the Babylonian god of the moon). NOTABLES: One of three young men, companions of Daniel, who were thrown into a fiery furnace after refusing to bow down and worship Nebuchadnezzar's golden idol (Daniel 1:7, 2:49, 3:12–30) VARIATIONS: Shad, Shadrack.

A Walk in a Fiery Furnace: A Story of Shadrach

King Nebuchadnezzar, who ruled over the enormous empire of Babylon, ordered his people to build a golden statue of a Babylonian god. The gigantic statue stood nearly one hundred feet tall. When the work was completed, Nebuchadnezzar invited all his provincial governors, judges, important leaders, and wise men for the festivities. For the installation, he arranged for musicians to play their instruments at the ceremonies. When people heard the music begin to be played, they were to kneel and pray to the great metal statue. Anyone refusing to do so would be thrown into a fiery furnace.

The music began and people fell to their knees . . . all except Daniel's three friends, Hananiah, Mishael, and Azariah, whose Babylonian names were Shadrach, Meshach, and Abednigo. Daniel's friends were three young Israelites who had previously been captives of the Babylonians. But because Daniel was wise and became an interpreter of the king's dreams, he became an advisor to the monarch. On the day of the statue's investiture, Daniel was away seeing to the king's business.

The field containing the statue was full that day with subjects of the king, including astrologers, wise men, magicians, and enchanters. These seers hated the Jews, especially Daniel, because he could do what they could not—provide the right interpretation of Nebuchadnezzar's troubling dreams. Local Babylonians, who had lost their powerful positions to Daniel and his friends, couldn't help telling the king how the Jews refused to bow down before the idol.

Nebuchadnezzar had the men seized and brought before him. He asked the men why they had not bowed down when in all other ways they had served him well. He gave them a final chance to reconsider. They could either bow before the Babylonian idol or burn to death in a furnace. The young Israelites told the king that they had respect for him but their God was a higher power. They were confident that even if they were thrown into a blazing furnace their Lord would protect them. But even if he did not, they could never bow before the statue of a pagan god in the field.

Nebuchadnezzar could not bear such defiance and ordered the servants to stoke the fire of the furnace so that it would become the hottest fire on earth. The fire eventually glowed white and the furnace was ready. The men were bound and then pushed into the blaze. The fire was so intense that the guards who were responsible for escorting the Israelites into the flames were overcome by the heat and fell dead at the opening.

Nebuchadnezzar shouted that he could see four people inside the furnace walking around, their hands no longer bound. The fourth person looked like no one he had ever seen. It must have struck fear into the heart of the king to see such a miraculous sight, for he called forth to the three men to come out of the furnace.

The crowd pushed in to see the three Israelites and not one had a single hair on his head burned. Their clothes had not been scorched. They did not have the scent of smoke anywhere upon them.

Nebuchadnezzar began to praise the God of the Israelites for sending an angel to save them from death. He told everyone that the men had so much faith in their God that they could defy the King of Babylon and face death rather than fall before any other god. He decreed on that day that no one was permitted to disparage the God of the Israelites. He promoted Daniel's friends to high positions of authority within the empire.

SHALOM *(Hebrew)* Peace. VARIATIONS: Sholom.

SHAUL *(Hebrew)* Form of Saul.

SHEM *(Hebrew)* Famous.

SHEMEI *(Hebrew)* Hearing and obeying the Lord. NOTABLES: The name of a number of different men in the Old Testament, including a brother of King David (2 Samuel 21:21). VARIATIONS: Schimei, Shimeah, Shimhi.

SHILHI *(Hebrew)* Bough; armor; weapon. NOTABLES: The name of Jehoshaphat's maternal grandfather. Shilhi's daughter was Azubah (1 Kings 22:42).

SHILLEM *(Hebrew)* Requital; peace; retribution. NOTABLES: One of the sons of Naphtali, descendant of Jacob (Genesis 46:24).

SHILOH *(Hebrew)* Peace; abundance; gift from God. VARIATIONS: Shilo.

SHIMON *(Hebrew)* Heard. NOTABLES: Father of four boys who are listed in one of the genealogies of the tribe of Judah (1 Chronicles 4:20). VARIATIONS: Simeon.

SHIMRON *(Hebrew)* Watchful. NOTABLES: Issachar's fourth son (Genesis 46:13).

SHLOMO *(Hebrew)* Peace.

SHMUEL *(Hebrew)* Form of Samuel.

SIDON *(Arabic)* Name of the main city in ancient Phoenicia that is now located in Lebanon. VARIATIONS: Zidon, Saïda.

SIMA *(Hebrew)* Treasure.

SIMCHA *(Hebrew)* Joy.

SIMEON *(Hebrew)* Hearing.

SIMON *(Hebrew)* God hears. NOTABLES: Biblical figure who, with his brother Levi, attacked the Shechemites to avenge his sister Dinah's rape by a Shechem prince (Genesis 34: 2, 25, 26). VARIATIONS: Simeon, Simion, Simm, Simms, Simone, Symms, Symon.

SOL *(Hebrew)* Short form of Solomon.

SOLOMON *(Hebrew)* Peaceable. NOTABLES: Biblical king famous for his wisdom. VARIATIONS: Salamen, Salamon, Salamun, Salaun, Salman, Salmon, Salom, Salomo, Salomon, Salomone, Selim, Shelomoh, Shlomo, Sol, Solaman, Sollie, Solly, Soloman, Solomo, Solomonas, Solomone.

STEPHEN *(Greek)* Crown. NOTABLES: Disciple of Jesus who became the first Christian martyr (Acts 7:59).

The Stoning of Stephen, First Christian Martyr

Stephen, a Jewish follower of Jesus, possessed an incisive and logical mind and the gift of eloquent speech. He was one of a group of seven honorable men chosen to oversee his congregation's proper distribution of food to the poor. A problem arose when some Greek-speaking widows complained that they were not being given their fair share of food when it was handed out. The Apostles heard their complaint but were too busy to deal with it themselves each day, so they chose an oversight group to resolve the problem. The group of men included Stephen, Philip, Procorus, Nicanor, Timon, Parmenas, and Nicolas. The men were prayed over by The Apostles so that they might serve the poor to the best of their abilities. The Apostles then had time to do their work of spreading the gospel to more potential followers of Christ.

During the Apostles' lifetime, the Holy Spirit imparted many gifts upon the Apostles and Jesus' followers. Stephen performed miracles and preached forcefully. He was a formidable foe to his opponents, who were no match for his wisdom. Some Jews spoke against Stephen and falsely accused him of speaking disrespectfully about Moses and God. The high priest ordered Stephen to appear before the members of the Sanhedrin.

The false witnesses against Stephen lied to the high priest and said that he had blasphemed the law, the temple, and the keepers of the law, the priests. The high priest demanded to know if the charges were true. Stephen took his time in answering the charges. He beautifully articulated the history of the Jewish people and the building and collapse of their nation. He explained that Jesus was part of God's divine plan for his children.

Stephen's words fell on deaf ears. He intensified his rhetoric, asking them if there was ever a prophet that their fathers did not persecute. He told them that they even killed those seers who prophesied the coming of Jesus. They had even murdered Jesus. You "have received the law by the disposition of angels, and have not kept it" (Acts 7:53).

The priests were outraged. They bit him and dragged him out of the city and stoned him. Stephen prayed as he was being stoned. He asked the Lord not to hold their sin against them. With those final words, he entered the deep sleep of death. Standing near Stephen to watch the martyrdom of the first Christian apostle was a young Saul of Tarsus. His eyewitness account would one day be contained in the Bible's Acts of the Apostles.

T

TAL *(Hebrew)* Rain.

TALON *(Hebrew)* Claw.

TARSHISH *(Hebrew)* Examination; contemplation. NOTABLES: One of the descendants of Noah born after the flood (Genesis 10:4).

TARSUS *(Hebrew/Greek)* Winged or feathered; city in ancient Greece where the Apostle Paul was born. He was a Jew who was also a Roman citizen.

TAVARES *(Aramaic)* Misfortune. VARIATIONS: Tavor.

TELEM *(Hebrew)* Furrow.

TERACH *(Hebrew)* Goat. VARIATIONS: Tera, Terah.

TERTULLUS *(Latin)* Roman clan name that possibly means "smooth." VARIATIONS: Tarrance, Terencio, Terrance, Terrence, Terrey, Terri, Terry.

TEVA *(Hebrew)* Nature.

THADDEUS *(Aramaic)* Brave; Greek form is Theudas. NOTABLES: One of the twelve Apostles chosen and commissioned to spread the message of Christianity (Matthew 10:1–4). VARIATIONS: Taddeo, Tadeo, Tadio, Thad, Thaddaus.

THANIEL *(Hebrew)* Form of Nathaniel.

THOMAS *(Aramaic)* Twin. NOTABLES: Jesus' doubting disciple (John 20:27). VARIATIONS: Tam, Tameas, Thom, Thompson, Thomson, Thumas, Tom, Tomas, Tomaso, Tomasso, Tomaz, Tomcio, Tomek, Tomelis, Tomi, Tomie, Tomislaw, Tomm, Tommy, Tomsen, Tomson, Toomas, Tuomas, Tuomo.

TIBERIAS *(Hebrew/Latin)* Son of Tiberias.

TIM *(English)* Form of Timothy. VARIATIONS: Timm, Tym, Tymm.

TIMMY *(English)* Form of Timothy.

TIMOTHEUS *(Greek)* Honoring God. NOTABLES: Associate of the Apostle Paul mentioned in 1 Thessalonians 1:1.

TIMOTHY *(Greek)* Honoring God. Form of Timotheus. NOTABLES: Young Christian missionary who watched over the church in Ephesus and to whom the Apostle Paul wrote two letters contained in the New Testament (1 and 2 Timothy). VARIATIONS: Timo, Timofeo, Timon, Timoteo, Timothe, Timotheo, Timotheus, Timothey, Tymmothy, Tymothy.

TIMUN *(Greek)* God-fearing.

TIRAS *(Hebrew)* Crushing. NOTABLES: One of the Biblical descendants of Noah born after the flood (Genesis 10:2).

TISHBITE *(Hebrew)* That captivates. NOTABLES: Biblical reference to Elijah the Tishbite (1 Kings 17:1, 21:17, 28).

TITUS *(Greek)* Of the giants. VARIATIONS: Tito, Titos.

TIVON *(Hebrew)* Lover of nature.

TOAH *(Hebrew)* Weapon; dart.

TOBIAH *(Hebrew)* Form of Tobias. NOTABLES: Son of Tobit assisted by an angel calling himself Azariah as he tried to avoid death and take a wife. The story appears in the Book of Tobit in Catholic Bibles.

Tobiah Takes a Wife

Sarah, the daughter of Raguel, had married seven times but was still a virgin. She was a pretty and sensuous creature and her would-be husbands each loved her. However, seven times Sarah had endured the trauma of her bridegrooms dying on the wedding night. Sarah was loved not only by her husbands but also by a demon that would not permit the bridegroom to consummate his marriage to Sarah. Though the blame for the deaths was not hers to bear, nevertheless, she was ostracized and scorned. The young woman wanted to die.

The eighth man destined to marry Sarah was Tobiah, the son of a man named Tobit. Tobit, known for his piety and devotion to the Lord, was blind. An angel of the Lord came to the house where Tobit and Tobiah lived. The angel called himself Azariah. Tobiah and Azariah walked along until they came to a river where a fish leaped out of the water and attempted to latch onto Tobiah's foot. The angel told the young man to catch the fish, remove its heart, gall, and liver, and preserve them. He explained that while the gall could be used to cure blindness, the other two organs could be burned to get rid of demons.

That night Tobiah and Azariah planned to stop at Raguel's house. The angel would ask for Sarah's hand in marriage to Tobiah. Sarah's father would not object because Tobiah was a kinsman.

Tobiah and Azariah arrive on time at Raguel's where Sarah and Raguel's wife, Edna, met them. Raguel asked about Tobit. When Tobiah spoke of his father's blindness, everyone wept. The conversation moved toward the marriage proposition. Raguel agreed that Sarah should be Tobiah's wife. He told the young man and the angel the fate of the previous bridegrooms. He produced a scroll for the wedding contract, and the parties agreed to the arrangement.

Raguel instructed his workers to dig a grave even as he made ready for a wedding. That way, when Tobiah died, he could quietly be put away. No one need ever know. Raguel surely wanted to spare Sarah further scorn.

Before crawling into bed with Sarah, Tobiah burned some incense and placed the fish heart and liver upon the embers. The stench was so terrible that it drove the demon into the desert of Upper Egypt.

Tobiah and his wife first prayed on their wedding night then made love. The next day the servant found the sleeping couple, both alive. Sarah's parents fell to the ground and praised God, then ordered the servants to put the dirt back into the grave. Sarah's family prepared a massive wedding feast of steers and rams and loaves of bread. Tobiah stayed with the family for fourteen days. When he left with Sarah, Raguel gave him half of all he owned. The other half would be given to him when Raguel and Edna passed away.

When Tobiah reached home, he rubbed the eyes of his aged father with the gall of the fish and pinched off the cataracts, ending his father's blindness.

TOBIAS *(Hebrew)* God is good. VARIATIONS: Tobe, Tobey, Tobia, Tobiah, Tobie, Tobin, Toby.

TODOR *(Greek)* Gracious gift.

TOGERMAH *(Hebrew)* Rugged. NOTABLES: One of the descendants of Noah born after the flood (Genesis 10:3).

TRINITY *(Latin)* The Holy Trinity.

TUBAL *(Hebrew)* Production. NOTABLES: One of the descendants of Noah born after the flood (Genesis 10:2).

TYCHICUS *(Greek)* Chance. NOTABLES: Christian man called a beloved brother, faithful minister, and fellow servant in the Lord by the Apostle Paul (Colossians 4:7).

U

URI *(Hebrew)* God's light. VARIATIONS: Uria, Uriah, Urias, Urie, Uriel.

URIAH *(Hebrew)* My light.

UZIEL *(Hebrew)* Powerful. VARIATIONS: Uzziel.

UZZA *(Hebrew)* My strength; power. NOTABLES: Son of Ehud and a descendant of King Saul (1 Chronicles 8:7, 13:10).

UZZIAH *(Hebrew)* God is my strength. VARIATIONS: Ozias, Uzia, Uziah, Uziya, Uzziah.

V

VIC *(Latin)* Form of Victor.

VICTOR *(Latin)* Conqueror. VARIATIONS: Vic, Vick, Victoir, Victorien, Victorino, Victorio, Viktor, Vitenka, Vitor, Vittore, Vittorio, Vittorios.

VINCENT *(Latin)* Victor; conqueror.

VITAS *(Latin)* Vital. VARIATIONS: Vitus.

X

XERXES *(Persian)* Ruler. NOTABLES: Believed to have been the man destined to be the richest and most powerful of the ancient Persian kings as foreseen by Daniel although Daniel did not specifically reveal the king's name (Daniel 11:2).

Y

YADID *(Hebrew)* Beloved.

YADIN *(Hebrew)* God will judge. VARIATIONS: Yadon.

YAKIM *(Hebrew)* God develops. VARIATIONS: Jakim.

YECHEZKEL *(Hebrew)* God strengthens. VARIATIONS: Chaskel, Chatzkel, Keskel.

YEHOSHUA *(Hebrew)* God is salvation. VARIATIONS: Yeshua.

YEHOYAKIM *(Hebrew)* God will establish. VARIATIONS: Jehoiakim, Yehoiakim, Yoyakim.

YEHUDI *(Hebrew)* A man from Judah; someone who is Jewish. VARIATIONS: Yechudi.

YERED *(Hebrew)* To come down. VARIATIONS: Jered.

YERIEL *(Hebrew)* Founded by God. VARIATIONS: Jeriel.

YISRAEL *(Hebrew)* Israel.

YITRO *(Hebrew)* Plenty. VARIATIONS: Yitran.

YITZCHAK *(Hebrew)* Laughter. VARIATIONS: Itzhak, Yitzhak.

YONATAN *(Hebrew)* Gift from God.

YOSEF *(Hebrew)* God increases. VARIATIONS: Yoseff, Yosif, Yousef, Yusef, Yusif, Yusuf, Yuzef.

YOSHA *(Hebrew)* Wisdom.

YUVAL *(Hebrew)* Brook. VARIATIONS: Jubal.

Z

ZABAD *(Hebrew)* Present. NOTABLES: Son of Ephraim, was slain by the men of Gath, who wanted his cattle (1 Chronicles 7:21). VARIATIONS: Zavad.

ZACCHEUS *(Hebrew)* Pure.

ZACHARIAH *(Hebrew)* The Lord has remembered. VARIATIONS: Zacaria, Zacarias, Zach, Zacharia, Zacharias, Zachary, Zachery, Zack, Zackariah, Zackerias, Zackery, Zak, Zakarias, Zakarie, Zako, Zeke.

ZADOK *(Hebrew)* Righteous.

ZAHAVI *(Hebrew)* Gold.

ZAHIR *(Hebrew)* Bright. VARIATIONS: Zaheer, Zahur.

ZAIDE *(Hebrew)* Older.

ZAKAI *(Hebrew)* Pure. VARIATIONS: Zaki, Zakkai.

ZAKUR *(Hebrew)* Masculine. VARIATIONS: Zaccur.

ZALMAN *(Hebrew)* Peaceful.

ZAMIR *(Hebrew)* Song.

ZAN *(Hebrew)* Well fed.

ZARAD *(Hebrew)* Ambush.

ZARAH *(Hebrew)* Brightness; east.

ZARED *(Hebrew)* Trap.

ZAREEF *(Arabic)* Elegant.

ZAVDIEL *(Hebrew)* Gift from God. VARIATIONS: Zabdiel, Zebedee.

ZEBADIAH *(Hebrew)* Gift from God. VARIATIONS: Zeb, Zebediah.

ZEBAH *(Hebrew)* Victim; sacrifice; deprived of protection.

ZEBEDEE *(Greek)* Form of Zebadiah.

ZEBULUN *(Hebrew)* To exalt. NOTABLES: Son of Jacob and Leah. Zebulun was the leader of one of the twelve tribes of Israel. VARIATIONS: Zebulen, Zebulon.

ZEDEKIAH *(Hebrew)* God is just. VARIATIONS: Tzedekia, Tzidkiya, Zed, Zedechiah, Zedekia, Zedekias.

ZE'EV *(Hebrew)* Wolf.

ZEHARIAH *(Hebrew)* Light of God. VARIATIONS: Zeharia, Zeharya.

ZEKE *(Hebrew)* The strength of God.

ZELIG *(Hebrew)* Holy.

ZEMARIAH *(Hebrew)* Song. VARIATIONS: Zemaria, Zemarya.

ZEPHANIAH *(Hebrew)* Protection. VARIATIONS: Zeph, Zephan.

ZERACH *(Hebrew)* Light. VARIATIONS: Zerachia, Zerachya, Zerah.

ZERAHIAH *(Hebrew)* Whom Jehovah caused to rise.

ZEREM *(Hebrew)* Stream.

ZERIKA *(Hebrew)* Rain shower.

ZEUS *(Greek)* Living; king of the gods. VARIATIONS: Zeno, Zenon, Zinon.

ZEV *(Hebrew)* Short form of Zebulun.

ZEVACH *(Hebrew)* Sacrifice. VARIATIONS: Zevachia, Zevachtah, Zevachya, Zevah.

ZEVADIAH *(Hebrew)* God bestows. VARIATIONS: Zevadia, Zevadya.

ZEVID *(Hebrew)* Present.

ZEVULUN *(Hebrew)* House. VARIATIONS: Zebulon, Zebulun, Zevul.

ZICHRI *(Hebrew)* That remembers.

ZIMRA *(Hebrew)* Sacred. VARIATIONS: Zemora, Zimrat, Zimri, Zimriah.

ZINDEL *(Hebrew)* Protector of mankind. VARIATIONS: Zindil.

ZION *(Hebrew)* Guarded land. VARIATIONS: Tzion, Zyon.

ZIPH *(Hebrew)* Falsehood.

ZISKIND *(Yiddish)* Sweet child.

ZITHRI *(Hebrew)* Protection of Jehovah.

ZIV *(Hebrew)* To shine. VARIATIONS: Zivan, Zivi.

ZOHAR *(Hebrew)* Bright light.

ZOLLY *(Hebrew)* Form of Solly (Solomon). VARIATIONS: Zollie, Zolio.

ZOMEIR *(Hebrew)* One who prunes trees. VARIATIONS: Zomer.

ZURIEL *(Hebrew)* The Lord is my rock.

ZVI *(Hebrew)* Deer.

Part Two

girl
names

A

AALIYAH *(Arabic)* Highest; most exalted one.

ABBI *(Arabic)* Great.

ABELIA *(Assyrian)* Child. VARIATIONS: Abella, Bella, Bell.

ABI *(Hebrew)* One who is exalted. Short form of Abjihah.

ABIA *(Arabic)* Great. NOTABLES: Biblical mother of Hezekiah, king of Judah, and daughter of Zechariah (2 Kings 18:1–2). VARIATIONS: Abi, Abbi, Abbey.

ABIAH *(Hebrew)* Highest; most exalted one.

ABIGAIL *(Hebrew)* My father is joy; cause of joy. NOTABLES: Biblical widow who became the wife of King David after her husband Nabal died (1 Samuel 25:2–3, 39). VARIATIONS: Abigayle, Gail.

Abigail Saves Her Husband

Abigail was beautiful, smart, and enterprising. Her husband, Nabal, of the house of Caleb was "churlish and evil" (1 Samuel 25:3). Abigail was thought to have been generous and warm-hearted while her husband was self-focused and uncouth. Some might say they were a mismatched pair. Still, they married and made a life with each other in the hills of southern Judea in the town of Maon. Among his holdings, Nabal had 3,000 sheep and 1,000 goats. By the yardsticks of that time, the couple was fairly prosperous. The future King David even provided security for their animals in Carmel at sheep-shearing time.

One day while Nabal was shearing his sheep near Carmel, David learned that he was in the vicinity. David was there with his men. They were thirsty and needed food. David recalled his friend Nabal and decided to ask him for food and drink. He sent his young messengers to his old friend.

Nabal either had forgotten about his relationship with David or did not want to have to stop his work to show any generosity. He said, "Who is David? And who is the son of Jesse? There be many servants now a days that break away every man from his master. Shall I then take my bread, and my water, and my flesh that I have killed for my shearers, and give it unto men, whom I know not whence they be?" (1 Samuel 25:10–11)

David's messengers returned empty-handed and they shared with their leader Nabal's words. David took a bold and decisive course of action. Accompanied by 400 soldiers outfitted with swords, he headed toward the place where Nabal was working with the sheep.

A servant went to Abigail with David's plan. The woman knew that her husband's hours were running out and if she didn't do something quickly, his head would be cut off. In a small amount of time, she gathered a large amount of food and an equal quantity of wine for a banquet she and her servants would provide David and his men. It took a caravan of donkeys to carry it all. As soon as she caught sight of David, she fell at his feet to demonstrate her deep respect for him. She had not consulted with her husband before undertaking such a course of action. She did ask him if she could use all the resources she needed for the meal. Abigail offered David food and some wine. She asked forgiveness for Nabal, telling David to put the blame upon her. It seemed silly to kill such a churlish and coarse man. Fortunately for Nabal, David changed his mind about killing Abigail's husband.

Soon afterward, Abigail sought Nabal to tell him of what she had done. He was drunk and hosting a great feast in their house. She decided to put off telling him until the next morning. When the sun came up the next day, Abigail went to Nabal and told him the whole story. The man went rigid like a stone. Ten days later, he died. After his death, David sent messengers to Abigail. He wanted to know if she would be his wife. Abigail decided to marry David. She bore him a son named Chileab (2 Samuel 3:2–3). The boy was also called Daniel (1 Chronicles 3:1). Abigail's new husband became king.

ABIJAH *(Hebrew)* Highest; one who is exalted. NOTABLES: Biblical woman who was Zechariah's daughter (2 Chronicles 29:1).

ABISHAG *(Hebrew)* Of error; ignorance of the father. NOTABLES: Shunemmite girl who kept King David's old and frail body warm at night (1 Kings 1:1–3).

A Virgin's Body Warms an Old King: A Story of Abishag

When King David had grown old and weak, his body could not generate much heat and he often felt cold. His servants decided to scour the land for a young virgin who could be their ruler's companion by day and lie next to him at night to warm his body. After an exhaustive search, they found Abishag the Shunem-mite. The lovely young woman must have agreed to the arrangement, for the Bible states that "the damsel was very fair, and cherished the king, and ministered to him, but the king knew her not" (1 Kings 1:4). The phrase "knew her not" implies that they did not have an intimate physical relationship.

ABITAL *(Hebrew)* Of dew. NOTABLES: Biblical mother of Shephatiah (2 Samuel 3:4).

ACHSAH *(Hebrew)* The Lord is my God. NOTABLES: Daughter of Caleb, who offered her as a wife to the man who could overpower the town of Kirjath-sepher, in the Judean hill country south of Hebron, and take it (Joshua 15:16).

ADAH *(Hebrew)* Adornment. NOTABLES: Wife of Esau, daughter of Elon the Hittite (Genesis 36:2).

ADALIA *(Hebrew)* God as protector.

ADARA *(Greek)* Lovely woman.

ADINA *(Hebrew)* Delicate; adorned; voluptuous; dainty. VARIATIONS: Adeana, Adin, Adine.

ADONIAH *(Hebrew)* The Lord is my God. VARIATIONS: Adon, Adonia, Adonijah, Adoniya, Adoniyah.

ADORA *(Latin)* Much adored. VARIATIONS: Adoree, Adoria, Adorlee, Dora, Dori, Dorie, Dorrie.

ADORABELLA *(Latin)* Adored beauty.

ADRIEL *(Hebrew)* God's flock.

AFRA *(Hebrew)* Young doe. VARIATIONS: Aphra.

AGATHA *(Greek)* Good. VARIATIONS: Aga, Agace, Agacia, Agafia, Agasha, Agata, Agate, Agathe, Agathi, Agatta, Ageneti, Aggi, Aggie, Aggy, Akeneki.

AGRIPPINA *(Latin)* Born feet first. VARIATIONS: Agrafina, Agrippine.

AHAVA *(Hebrew)* Beloved; essence; being; generation. VARIATIONS: Ahavah, Ahavat, Ahouva, Ahuda, Ahuva.

AHINOAM *(Hebrew)* Of grace; beauty of the brother. NOTABLES: Biblical woman who was the wife of Saul (1 Samuel 14:50); also the name of a woman from Jezreel who became the third wife of David (1 Samuel 25:43).

Ahinoam, One of the Many Wives of David

Before and after David became King of Judah, he took ten wives and a concubine that the Bible lists in the genealogy of David. But he had other wives, concubines, and children, some named and some not named in the Bible (2 Samuel 5:13). David acquired his first wife, Michal, the daughter of King Saul, after he killed one hundred Philistines.

David met Ahinoam of Jezreel while living somewhat like a fugitive, trying to stay clear of King Saul and his men. Not much is known about Ahinoam, who became David's wife after Michal. However,

Ahinoam gave David his firstborn son, a child they named Amnon (2 Samuel 3:2). The name in Hebrew means "faithful and true."

AHOLAH *(Hebrew)* She who has her own tent.

AHOLIBAMAH *(Hebrew)* Tent of the high place; my tabernacle is exalted. NOTABLES: Wife of Esau, daughter of Anah (Genesis 36:2). VARIATIONS: Oholibamah.

Aholibamah Bears Three Sons

Esau had not married Hebrew women. He took his wives from the Canaanites. After Esau and his brother Jacob parted ways, Esau moved his wives, children, cattle, and servants to another land away from Canaan and Jacob. The place where Esau went was known as Mount Seir. It was there that Esau, his family, and the group of people who went with him settled.

While he yet lived in Canaan, he had chosen Aholibamah, the daughter of Anah, as a wife. Not much is known about her. She was one of three wives belonging to Esau. The others were Adah and Basemath. With these three women, Esau had many sons. While she and her husband still lived in Canaan, Aholibamah gave birth to sons Jeush and Jaalam and Korah. Esau and his sons had God's blessing even though they had left the land of the Israelites. They became the Edomites and, in time, showed themselves to be an important group of people who were neighbors of the Israelites. Edom means "red" in Hebrew. God blessed Esau and, according to the second chapter of Deuteronomy, he forbade the Israelites to fight the Edomites. While Canaan was the Promised Land that God wanted Jacob to have, Mount Seir (named for the descendants of Seir, the Horite, who lived there) became the land that the Lord of Abraham allowed the Edomites to possess. (Genesis 36:20).

AKILA *(Egyptian)* Intelligent.

AKILI *(Arabic)* Wisdom.

ALETHIA *(Greek)* Truth. VARIATIONS: Alathea, Alathia, Aleethia, Aletea, Aletha, Alethia, Alithea, Alithia.

ALISA *(Hebrew)* Happiness. VARIATIONS: Alisah, Alisanne, Alissa, Alissah, Aliza, Allisa, Allisah, Allissa, Allissah, Allyea, Allysah, Alyssa, Alyssah.

ALIYAH *(Hebrew/Arabic)* Exalted; going up. VARIATIONS: Aaliyah, Aliya, Aliye, Allyah, Alya.

ALIZA *(Hebrew)* Joyful. VARIATIONS: Alitza, Alitzah, Aliz, Alizka.

ALONA *(Hebrew)* Oak tree; strong. VARIATIONS: Allona, Allonia, Alonia, Eilonia.

ALPHA *(Greek)* First letter of the Greek alphabet. VARIATIONS: Alfa.

ALTA *(Latin)* High. VARIATIONS: Allta.

ALTHEA *(Greek)* Healer. VARIATIONS: Altha, Althaia, Altheta, Althia.

ALTHEDA *(Greek)* Blossom.

AMADEA *(Latin)* Loved by God.

AMANI *(Arabic)* Hopes; dreams; wishes.

AMARE *(Latin)* Beloved.

AMARIS *(Hebrew)* Covenant with God. VARIATIONS: Amaria, Amariah.

AMARISA *(Hebrew)* Given by God.

AMBROCIO *(Greek)* Immortal.

AMIDA *(Hebrew)* Moral. VARIATIONS: Amidah.

ANAH *(Hebrew)* Answer.

ANAHELLA *(Latin)* Graceful; beautiful.

ANAIS *(Hebrew)* Graceful.

ANALISE *(Hebrew)* Committed to God.

ANAT *(Egyptian/Hebrew)* To sing.

ANCILLA *(Latin)* Handmaiden.

ANGELA *(Greek)* Heavenly messenger.

ANGELITA *(Greek)* Messenger.

ANIM *(Hebrew)* Answerings; afflictions; singings.

ANINA *(Hebrew)* Answer to a prayer.

ANN *(Hebrew)* Gracious. NOTABLES: Mother of the Blessed Virgin Mary and wife of Joachim, forebear of God (as the earthly father of the Virgin Mary is referred to by the Catholic church). The stories of Ann and Joachim are found in the apocryphal proto-gospel of James.

ANNA *(Hebrew)* Grace; form of Hannah. NOTABLES: Prophetess and widowed daughter of Phanuel who praised young Jesus when his parents brought him to Temple (Luke 2:36–38).

ANNUNCIATA *(Latin)* Announcement; annunciation.

ANONA *(Latin)* Harvest of grain.

ANTIOCHIS *(Latin)* Feminine form of Antiochus. NOTABLES: Concubine of Antiochus IV Epiphanies, who gave her the towns of Tarsus and Mallos (2 Maccabees 4:30).

ANTOINETTA *(Latin)* Praiseworthy.

ANTONIA *(Latin)* Beyond price. VARIATIONS: Antonea.

APOLLONIA *(Greek)* Strength. NOTABLES: Name of the town that the Apostle Paul passed through on his way to Thessalonica (Acts 17:1). VARIATIONS: Apolinara, Apolinia, Apoline.

APPHIA *(Greek)* Increasing. NOTABLES: Christian who served the early church and befriended the Apostle Paul (Philemon 1:2).

Apphia and Philemon, Friends of the Apostle Paul

Apphia is mentioned in the New Testament in a letter written by the Apostle Paul to her husband Philemon. He addressed Apphia as "beloved" and gave a greeting to Archippus. Archippus may have been Apphia and Philemon's son or a brother. Some sources suggest he may have been a minister in a Christian church, possibly at Colossae. Apphia and her family were Christians and the congregation met in Philemon's house. They may have been evangelized and converted by Paul.

The letter to Philemon was written while Paul was in prison. Philemon was wealthy. He owned slaves in Colossae. One of his slaves was a runaway named Onesimus who had taken whatever items he could put his hands on (Philemon 1:18). Paul wrote to Philemon to ask him, as a brother in Christ, to consider the fate of Onesimus. If the slave had taken things and wronged him, Paul asked Philemon to put it on Paul's account and he would repay it.

Paul wanted Philemon to look upon Onesimus as a Christian and treat him accordingly. He asked Philemon to see Onesimus as a helper. Many wealthy people owned slaves during ancient times, but as Paul wrote: "For as many of you as have been baptized into Christ have put on Christ. There is neither Jew nor Greek, there is neither bond nor free, there is neither male nor female: for ye are all one in Christ Jesus" (Galatians 3:27–28).

Paul may have hoped that Philemon would forgive Onesimus and that his friend's Christian values would prevail over common cultural practices. However, Philemon would be taking a risk, because a slave uprising could have been the consequence of making an example of Onesimus. Is it possible that Paul could have wanted Onesimus returned to him? The fate of Onesimus is not known. Tradition states that with the increase in anti-Christian sentiment, Paul's beloved friend Apphia and her husband and son were imprisoned and ultimately suffered death by stoning.

ARAMINTA *(Hebrew)* High-minded; lofty. VARIATIONS: Araminthe.

ARELLA *(Hebrew)* Angel. VARIATIONS: Arela.

ARETHA *(Greek)* Virtuous. VARIATIONS: Areta, Arethi, Arethusa, Aretina, Aretta, Arette.

ARIEL *(Hebrew)* Lioness of God. VARIATIONS: Aeriel, Aeriela, Ari, Ariela, Ariella, Arielle, Ariellel.

ARVA *(Latin)* From the seashore.

ASENATH *(Egyptian)* Gift of the sun-god; belonging to the goddess Neith *(Hebrew)* peril or misfortune. NOTABLES: Daughter of Potipherah, Priest of On, who was given as a wife to Joseph by Pharaoh (Genesis 41:45). VARIATIONS: Asnat.

ASHIRA *(Hebrew)* Wealthy. NOTABLES: Sherah, biblical daughter of Ephraim (1 Chronicles 7:24). VARIATIONS: Ashera, Shera, Sherah, Shira.

ASHNAH *(Hebrew)* Change.

ASHTORETH *(Hebrew)* Female demon of lust. VARIATIONS: Ashtoret.

ASTARTE *(Phoenician/Greek)* Fertility goddess. NOTABLES: Semitic goddess of war, fertility, and sexuality. Greeks accepted her as Aphrodite and the Romans called her Venus Erycina. VARIATIONS: Ashtart, Ashtoret.

ASTERA *(Hebrew)* Star. VARIATIONS: Asta, Asteria, Asteriya, Astra.

ATARAH *(Hebrew)* Crown. NOTABLES: Mother of Onam (1 Chronicles 2:26).

ATHALIA *(Hebrew)* Praise the Lord; afflicted of the Lord. NOTABLES: Biblical queen who eliminated the males of her royal family so she could assume the throne without threat (2 Kings 11.1). VARIATIONS: Atalia, Ataliah, Atalie, Atalya, Athalee, Athalie, Athalina.

AVITAL *(Hebrew)* Form of Abital.

AVIVA *(Hebrew)* Spring. VARIATIONS: Abiba, Abibah, Abibi, Abibit, Avivah, Avivi, Avivit.

AYELET *(Hebrew)* Deer.

AYLA *(Hebrew)* Oak tree.

AZARIAH *(Hebrew)* Helped by God. VARIATIONS: Azaria, Azelia.

AZRIELA *(Hebrew)* God is my strength; feminine form of Azriel. VARIATIONS: Azriella.

AZUBAH *(Hebrew)* Forsaken. Caleb's wife who had three sons (1 Chronicles 2:18–19) and mother of King Jehoshaphat (1 Kings 22:42).

B

BAPTISTA *(Greek)* Baptizer.

BARA *(Hebrew)* To choose. VARIATIONS: Bari, Barra.

BASEMATH *(Hebrew)* Fragrance; sweet scent.

BASHEMATH *(Hebrew)* Fragrant; pleasing. NOTABLES: Wife of Esau, daughter of Ishmael and sister of Nebajoth. She was also called Adah (Genesis 26:34, 36:2–3). VARIATIONS: Basemath, Bashmath, Basmath.

BASILIA *(Greek)* Royal. VARIATIONS: Basila, Basilea, Basilie

BATHIA *(Hebrew)* Daughter of God. VARIATIONS: Basha, Baspa, Batia, Batya, Bitya, Peshe, Pessel.

BATHSHEBA *(Hebrew)* Daughter of Sheba. NOTABLES: Wife of Uriah, whose death was arranged by King David. She became pregnant by the king and married him (2 Samuel 11:2–27).VARIATIONS: Bathseva, Batsheba, Batsheva, Batshua, Sheba.

BEATA *(Latin)* Blessed. VARIATIONS: Beate.

BECCA *(Hebrew)* Short form of Rebecca. VARIATIONS: Bekka.

BECHIRA *(Hebrew)* Chosen.

BEHIRA *(Hebrew)* Bright light.

BELLONA *(Latin)* Goddess of battle; goddess of war.

BENA *(Hebrew)* Wise.

BENICIA *(Latin)* Blessed one. VARIATIONS: Benecia.

BERNICE *(Greek)* Bringing victory. NOTABLES: Wife of King Agrippa (Acts 25:13). VARIATIONS: Berenice, Bernelle, Bernetta, Bernette, Bernicia, Bernie, Bernyce.

Bernice's name means victory, but there were moments in her life when she was less than victorious. In fact, there were episodes and events that were typified by moments of dark disappointment and reversals of fortune—and yet she became a queen.

She was the daughter of Herod Agrippa I. Her lineage was impressive—her great-grandfather was Herod I of Judea and her father was Herod Agrippa I, who was on friendly terms with Roman Emperor Claudius. She suffered disappointment in three marriages. Her first husband was a man named Marcus. Following that relationship, she married her uncle Herod, who was king of Chalcis. He died. She then married Ptolemy, king of Cilicia. Her marriage to him ensured her status as queen, but she apparently was not happy with him either, for she left to live with M. Julius Agrippa II, her brother. The brother and sister not only shared joint rulership over Galilee but also cohabited, allegedly, in an incestuous relationship.

Perhaps because she was beautiful and generous with gifts and seemed to be smitten with him, the aging emperor Vespasian was soon won over by Bernice. But perhaps she had an ulterior motive for focusing an interest on the old man, because it was Titus, the Roman general and Vespasian's son, to whom she gave her heart and soul. They became lovers when Bernice was forty and Titus was ten years younger in A.D. 69, according to Seutonius, a historian of that time. Other historians, including Tacitus and Josephus, wrote about her illicit dalliances, the strange relationship with Agrippa II, and the great love of her life, Titus.

About five years into her relationship with Titus, he wanted to marry her. However, Roman opinion decried such coupling because Bernice was Jewish and because the Jewish revolt in Jerusalem against the Romans was still fresh in the minds of the populace. Bernice went to Rome (in a.d. 75, according to some sources, although the date is disputed), where she lived as his concubine. Four years later, Titus became emperor and sent her away . . . a bitter ending of the relationship with the one man she loved more than all others.

BERURIA *(Hebrew)* Chosen by God.

BETH *(Hebrew)* House of God.

BETHANY *(Hebrew)* House of figs. NOTABLES: Place name in the New Testament; the location of the house where Mary, Martha, and Lazarus lived (John 11:1).

BETHEL *(Hebrew)* Temple; house of God. NOTABLES: Place name in southern Israel. Also known as Bethel, Bethuel, and Bethul; originally called Luz (Joshua 19:4; 1 Samuel 30:27; 1 Chronicles 4:30; Joshua 18:13).

BETHESDA *(Hebrew)* House of mercy.

BETHIA *(Hebrew)* Daughter of Jehovah. VARIATIONS: Betia, Bithia.

BETHSAIDA *(Aramaic)* House of hunting. NOTABLES: Place name where Andrew and Simon Peter, disciples of Jesus, lived, north of Lake Gennesaret (Mark 6:45, 53; John 1:44).

BETUEL *(Hebrew)* Daughter of God. VARIATIONS: Bethuel.

BETULAH *(Hebrew)* Dedicated. VARIATIONS: Bethula, Bethulah, Betula.

BEULAH *(Hebrew)* Married. VARIATIONS: Bealah, Beula.

BILHAH *(Hebrew)* Shy. NOTABLES: Slave girl who was the maidservant of Rachel who bore two sons to Jacob, Rachel's husband (Genesis 30:6–7).

BINA *(Hebrew)* Knowledge. VARIATIONS: Bena, Binah, Byna.

BINYAMINA *(Hebrew)* Right hand; feminine form of Benjamin.

BIRA *(Hebrew)* Fortress. VARIATIONS: Biria, Biriya.

BITHIAH *(Hebrew)* Yahweh's daughter. NOTABLES: Egyptian princess who was a Pharaoh's daughter and who married Mered, a member of the tribe of Judah.

BLIMA *(Hebrew)* Blossom. VARIATIONS: Blimah, Blime.

BLUM *(Hebrew)* Flower. VARIATIONS: Blithe, Blythe.

BRACHA *(Hebrew)* Blessing. VARIATIONS: Brocha.

BRANDA *(Hebrew)* Blessing.

BUTHAYNA *(Arabic)* Body of beauty.

C

CALISTA *(Greek)* Most beautiful. VARIATIONS: Cala, Calesta, Cali, Calissa, Calisto, Callie, Callista, Cally, Callysta, Calysta, Kala, Kallie.

CANDACE *(Latin)* White. VARIATIONS: Candice, Candie, Candis, Candiss, Candyce, Kandace, Kandice, Kandyce.

CANDRA *(Latin)* Radiant. VARIATIONS: Candria, Kandra.

CARMEL *(Hebrew)* Vineyard. VARIATIONS: Carmeli, Carmelina, Carmelita, Carmia, Carmiela, Carmit, Carmiya, Karma, Karmela, Karmella.

CARMI *(Hebrew)* Vine.

CASSANDRA *(Latin)* Unheeded prophetess. VARIATIONS: Cassey, Cassi, Cassie, Kasandra, Kasaundra.

CATHERINE *(English)* Pure. NOTABLES: Saint Catherine of Sienna, Saint Catherine of Genoa. VARIATIONS: Catalina, Catarina, Catarine, Cateline, Catharin, Catharine, Catharyna, Catharyne, Cathee, Cathelin, Cathelina, Cathelle, Catherin, Catherina, Catrin, Catrina, Catrine, Catryna, Kai, Kaitlin, Kata, Kataleen, Katerina, Katherine, Katheryn.

CHANA *(Hebrew)* Grace. VARIATIONS: Channa, Hannah.

CHANIA *(Hebrew)* Grace of the lord. VARIATIONS: Chaniya, Hania, Haniya.

CHARITY *(Latin)* Kindness. VARIATIONS: Charita, Charitee, Charitey, Sharitee.

CHASIA *(Hebrew)* Protected by God. VARIATIONS: Chasya, Hasia, Hasya.

CHASINA *(Hebrew)* Strong. VARIATIONS: Hasina.

CHASTITY *(Latin)* Purity. VARIATIONS: Chasta, Chastina, Chastine.

CHAVAH *(Hebrew)* To breathe.

CHAVIVAH *(Hebrew)* Beloved.

CHAVON *(Hebrew)* God is good. VARIATIONS: Chavona, Chavonna, Chavonne, Shavon.

CHAYAH *(Hebrew)* To live. VARIATIONS: Chabah, Chapka, Chavalah, Hava.

CHEMDIAH *(Hebrew)* God is my hope. VARIATIONS: Chemdia, Chemdiya, Hemdia, Hemdiah.

CHENIA *(Hebrew)* Grace of God. VARIATIONS: Chen, Chenya, Hen, Henia, Henya.

CHLOE *(Greek)* Green shoot; the summer name of the Greek goddess Demeter. NOTABLES: Christian woman who opened her home for worship (1 Corinthians 1:11).

CHRISTABEL *(Latin)* Beautiful Christian woman. VARIATIONS: Christabella, Christabelle, Cristabel, Cristabella.

CLARE *(Latin)* Bright; clear; shining. VARIATIONS: Claire, Clarisa, Clarissa, Clerissa.

CLAUDIA *(Latin)* Lame. VARIATIONS: Claudelle, Claudette, Claudina, Claudine.

CONCEPCION *(Latin)* Conception.

COZBI *(Hebrew)* Slipping away. NOTABLES: The Midianite princess that Phinehas slew to avert a plague (Numbers 25:6–15).

CYRENE *(Greek)* Siren. NOTABLES: Name of a Greek mythological water nymph that was loved by the God Apollo. VARIATIONS: Cyreen, Cyren, Cyrena.

D

DAGANA *(Hebrew)* Grain. VARIATIONS: Dagan, Degania, Deganya.

DALIT *(Hebrew)* Running water.

DALYA *(Hebrew)* Branch. VARIATIONS: Dalia, Daliya.

DAMARIS *(Greek)* Calf. VARIATIONS: Damara, Damaress, Dameris, Dameryss, Damiris.

DANAE *(Greek)* Pure and bright.

DANI *(Hebrew)* Short form of Danielle.

DANIAH *(Hebrew)* God's judgment. VARIATIONS: Dania, Daniya, Danya.

DANIELA *(Hebrew)* God is my judge. VARIATIONS: Daniella, Danyella.

DANYA *(Hebrew)* Judgment of the Lord.

DARA *(Hebrew)* Wisdom. VARIATIONS: Dahra, Dareen, Darice, Darissa, Darra.

DASSA *(Hebrew)* Form of Hadassah; myrtle tree.

DAVIDA *(Hebrew)* Beloved. Feminine version of David.

DAVINIA *(Latin)* Divine.

DEBORAH *(Hebrew)* Bee. NOTABLES: Nurse of Rebekah, Isaac's wife (Genesis 24:59; 35:8). Also, a Judge of Israel who calls herself "a mother in Israel" (Judges 5:7).

Deborah and Barak Emancipate the Israelites

The Israelites had fallen into wicked ways, so the Lord allowed them to be oppressed for twenty years by Jabin, the Canaanite king. Jabin's military commander was a man named Sisera. He oversaw an army with nine hundred iron chariots.

The Israelites prayed to God to have mercy on them. At that time, Israel had a judge and prophetess named Deborah who was married to Lapidoth and who held court under a palm tree between Bethel and Ramah. Deborah sent for Barak, whom she saw as someone who could help her rid the Israelites of the oppressive rule of Jabin. Barak was the son of Abinoam from Kedesh in Naphtali. She told him to send ten thousand men made up of the sons of Naphtali and the sons of Zebulun. She told Barak to put the men in position at the River Kishon and she would deliver Sisera into Barak's hands.

Barak told Deborah that he would go only if she would go with him. So she did, but first she told him a piece of prophecy—that is, that there would be no glory for him since "the Lord shall sell Sisera into the hand of a woman" (Judges 4:9).

Deborah went with Barak to Kedesh with Zebulun and Naphtali and ten thousand men. Sisera learned of the movement of the Israelites from Heber the Kenite, a distant descendant of the father-in-law of Moses. Heber the Kenite had pitched his tent a short distance away from a terebinth tree located near Kedesh. Sisera was told that Barak had taken some men up to Mount Tabor. Sisera rallied his troops along with the nine hundred chariots of iron and headed off to the River Kishon.

Barak followed Sisera's men and killed them all, but Sisera jumped on his chariot and fled. He caught sight of the tent of the wife of Heber the Kenite. The woman's name was Jael and she went outside her tent to meet Sisera. Her husband had a cordial relationship with Jabin, the king of Hazor. So Jael met Sisera and made him feel at ease. "Turn in, my lord, turn in to me; fear not. And when he had turned in unto her into the tent, she covered him with a mantle" (Judges 4:18).

Jael gave Sisera milk to drink and a blanket to cover himself. She stood guard at the door of the tent. Sisera relaxed and slept. Jael picked up a tent nail and a hammer and crept over to where Sisera was. She hammered the nail into his temple and he died.

Soon after Barak approached and Jael went to meet him. She told him to come into her tent and she would show him the man he was pursuing.

Deborah's prophecy proved true: Sisera was delivered into Barak's hands by a woman. Deborah and Barak composed a triumphal song in which Deborah referred to herself as a "mother in Israel" (Judges 5:7). The children of Israel understood that they had to grow stronger and more powerful until the day Jabin was defeated. But the battle led by Deborah and Barak certainly was a decisive victory in the war to defeat the oppressive rule of Jabin.

DEBRA *(Hebrew)* Short form of Deborah.

DELILAH *(Hebrew)* Delicate. NOTABLES: Samson's lover. She deceived him, cut his hair while he slept, and robbed him of his strength (Judges 16:4–21). VARIATIONS: Dalaiah, Dalila, Delaiah, Delila.

DEMETRA *(Greek)* Earth mother; variant of Demeter.

DEVORAH *(Hebrew)* Form of Deborah.

DIMONA *(Hebrew)* South. VARIATIONS: Demona, Demonah, Dimona.

DINAH *(Hebrew)* God will judge. NOTABLES: Biblical daughter born to Jacob and Leah (Genesis 30:20–21). VARIATIONS: Deena, Denora, Dina, Dinorah, Diondra, Dyna, Dynah.

The Price the Shechem Prince Pays for Dinah

Dinah, daughter of Leah and Jacob, had eleven brothers but no sisters. She and her brothers had the same father but her brothers had different mothers. Jacob's sons were born through his two wives, Leah and Rachel, and their maidservants. With so many men around, Dinah probably enjoyed being with other young women. She was pretty and inquisitive and enjoyed learning about new things, so one day her friends took her to a local nature festival in Shechem, near the land Jacob bought when he returned to Canaan. There a young prince called Shechem, the son of Hamor the Hevite, admired her. He believed himself to be in love with her and was so overcome by his burning desire for her that he took her and lay with her. Afterward, "his soul clave unto Dinah the daughter of Jacob, and he loved the damsel, and spake kindly unto the damsel. And Shechem spake unto his father Hamor, saying, Get me this damsel to wife" (Genesis 34:3–4).

The young man enlisted his father, the king, in helping to secure the young daughter of Jacob as his wife. But even before Hamor could sit down with Jacob and discuss the arrangement between the families, Jacob learned of the incident from his sons. Jacob remained measured, thoughtful, and quiet even though his sons were outraged and vocal because of the violation against their sister.

Hamor went to Jacob's house. He explained how his son had fallen in love with Dinah. He asked for permission for his son to marry her. Hamor even suggested that the two groups of people—the Hebrews and the Hevites—begin to intermarry. He offered a suitable dowry for the marriage between his son and Dinah, a fee that Jacob could keep even if he refused to allow the wedding to proceed.

Such a proposal required careful consideration. Jacob took his time . . . perhaps too much time, for his sons answered Shechem and Hamor for him. They told the two visitors that because Shechem had defiled Dinah, they would give her to him. But there was a condition. He and all the men in Shechem would have to be circumcised because their tradition would not allow Dinah, nor any Hebrew woman, to marry an uncircumcised male. Shechem and his father agreed, rose, and took Dinah to stay in their home as a guest (Genesis 34:17).

After three days when all the men in Shechem were finally circumcised but yet still weak and in pain, two of Dinah's brothers—Simeon and Levi—carried out their vengeful plan to kill all the Shechem men and the king in retaliation for making their sister a harlot. Dinah was removed from Shechem's home and taken back to Jacob's house. We'll never know if the brothers of Dinah used the incident between her and the Shechem prince as an excuse to claim all the Shechem land, but biblical scholars have raised that question. The sons of Jacob certainly displayed a youthful rashness and righteous sense of morality as they plotted against the Hevites. Their actions angered Jacob, in part because he feared such an action put his family and all their holdings in danger. Jacob reduces his son's portion of inherited lands. Dinah is not mentioned again in the Bible.

DIVINE *(Latin)* Divine. VARIATIONS: Divina, Divinia.

DIZA *(Hebrew)* Joy. VARIATIONS: Ditza, Ditzah.

DODIE *(Hebrew)* Beloved.

DOMINA *(Latin)* Woman. VARIATIONS: Domini.

DOR *(Aramaic)* Generation; span of time.

DORCAS *(Greek)* Gazelle. NOTABLES: Woman "full of good works" whose name of Tabitha (in Hebrew) was interpreted as Dorcas (Acts 9:36). VARIATIONS: Doreka.

DORIT *(Hebrew)* Generation. VARIATIONS: Dorrit.

DOROTHY *(Greek)* Gift from God. VARIATIONS: Dorethea, Doro, Dorotea, Dorotha, Dorothea, Dorothee.

DOVEVA *(Hebrew)* Graceful.

DRUSILLA *(Latin)* Mighty. NOTABLES: Wife of Felix who heard the Apostle Paul's testimony (Acts 24:24). VARIATIONS: Drucilla.

DULCE *(Latin)* Sweet. VARIATIONS: Delcina, Delcine, Delsine, Dulcea, Dulci, Dulcia, Dulciana, Dulcibella, Dulcibelle, Dulcina, Dulcine, Dulcinea.

DUMIA *(Hebrew)* Silent.

E

EDEN *(Hebrew)* Pleasure. VARIATIONS: Eaden, Eadin, Edana, Edena, Edenia, Edin, Edna, Ednah.

EGLAH *(Hebrew)* Heifer. NOTABLES: May be another name for Michal, wife of David.

EIDEL *(Yiddish)* Delicate.

EILAH *(Hebrew)* Oak tree. VARIATIONS: Aila, Ailah, Ala, Ayla, Eila, Eilona, Ela, Elona, Eyla.

ELAMA *(Hebrew)* God's people.

ELIANA *(Hebrew)* My prayers have been answered by God.

ELIEZRA *(Hebrew)* God is my salvation.

ELIORA *(Hebrew)* God is my light.

ELISABETH *(Hebrew)* God's promise. NOTABLES: Elisabeth, cousin of the Blessed Virgin Mary and mother of John the Baptist (Luke 1:36, 39–45). VARIATIONS: Babette, Bess, Bessie, Beth, Betsy, Bette, Bettie, Betty, Elisabet, Elisabetta, Elisabette, Eliza, Elizabeth, Elsbeth, Elspeth, Lib, Libbie, Libby, Libbye, Lis, Lisa, Lisbet, Liz, Lizbeth, Lizzie.

Elisabeth, Mother of John the Baptist

Elisabeth and Zacharias were pious Jews, advanced in years and without heirs. Elisabeth was the daughter of Elisheba and Aaron (Luke 1:5, 1:36). Some Bibles say she was a descendant of Aaron. Zacharias was a priest belonging to the class of Abijah. The couple longed for a child but had been unable to conceive. They kept the Law and all the commandments. They may also have been among the Jews who awaited the prophesied coming of the Messiah who would be the savior of the Hebrew people.

One day Zacharias was in the temple going about his priestly duties when he noticed a figure standing near. This was not an ordinary man. Although Jews were praying outside of the temple, inside, Zacharias was alone except for this being. It was the angel of the Lord, Gabriel, standing next to the altar of incense. Zacharias, upon seeing the angel of the Lord, felt apprehensive. From the angel, a calm serenity emanated. Gabriel told Zacharias that his elderly wife was with child. She would bear a son and they were to call him John (Luke 1:11–13).

Elisabeth was also told the good news. She and Zacharias were elated. Elisabeth was about six months into her pregnancy when her cousin Mary, who was pregnant with Jesus, made her way to the hills of Judah to the house of Elisabeth and Zacharias for a visit that would last three months (Luke 1:56). When Elisabeth opened the door to receive Mary, she immediately felt the presence of the Holy Spirit and praised Mary as the Mother of her Lord.

When it was her time to give birth, Elisabeth delivered a son, just as the angel had said she would. Eight days later, the newborn was circumcised and given his Hebrew name. Some who had gathered with Elisabeth and Zacharias for the joyous occasion thought that the baby should be given his father's name. Elisabeth did not want that. She insisted that they name him John. Relatives and friends all rejected that name because no one on either side of the family had ever had that name. They asked Zacharias what the child should be called. He had lost the ability to speak, so he wrote on a tablet the name "John." Upon doing that, the priest could speak again. The Bible says his tongue became loose and he could talk.

After his son was named, Zacharias was blessed by the Holy Spirit. He was filled with the power to prophesy. He foresaw that his child would be called a prophet of God and that he would prepare the way of the Messiah. John grew strong in spirit and became known as John the Baptist. The last of the biblical prophets, he would become Christ's first missionary. His death was by beheading by Herod Antipas.

ELISHA *(Hebrew)* Consecrated to God. VARIATIONS: Eleasha, Elecia, Eleesha, Elesha, Elysha.

ELISHEBA *(Hebrew)* God is my oath. NOTABLES: Sister of Naashon and daughter of Amminadab who married Aaron and bore him Nadab, Abihu, Eleazar, and Ithamar (Exodus 6:23).

ELISHEVA *(Hebrew)* Form of Elisheba; God is my oath.

ELIVAH *(Hebrew)* God is able.

ELKANA *(Hebrew)* Feminine form of Elkan or Elkanath. VARIATIONS: Elka, Elke, Elkie.

ELYSE *(Hebrew)* Consecrated to God. VARIATIONS: Elise, Elliza, Elsa, Else, Elsie.

EMUNA *(Hebrew)* Faithful.

EPHAH *(Hebrew)* Gloom. NOTABLES: Place name of an ancient city located near the Dead Sea and noted for its dates (Isaiah 60:6).

EPHRATAH *(Hebrew)* Abundance. NOTABLES: Wife of Caleb; an alternate name sometimes used in Judah for Bethlehem was Bethlehem-Ephratah (Micah 5:2) and its people were sometimes called

Ephrathites. Ephratah was where Rachel went into labor and perished giving birth to Benjamin (Genesis 35: 16–19).

ERELA *(Hebrew)* Angel.

ERLINDA *(Hebrew)* Spirit.

ESTHER *(Hebrew)* Star; happiness. NOTABLES: A Benjamite Jewess who risked her life for the cause of her people and captured the favor of the Persian king Ahasuerus. The king set aside his wife Vashti and made Esther his queen (Esther 2:17).

Esther Risks Her Life for Her People

The land once controlled by the Israelites fell under the rule of a powerful Persian king named Ahasuerus, also known as Xerxes. Xerxes decided to hold an extravagant party to display his wealth to his nobles and distinguished military leaders.

He invited all his friends into the palace gardens for a sumptuous banquet. The guests sipped wine from gold goblets, each uniquely decorated, and ate whatever they wanted because the king had ordered his servants to serve anything a guest desired.

Queen Vashti, wife of Xerxes, was having a party of her own for the women. The servants went to inform the queen that the king desired her presence "with the crown royal" (Esther 1:11). Now Vashti understood that she was to be on display wearing *only* the royal crown. She refused and sent the servants back. Xerxes became incensed. He would not tolerate a disobedient and disrespectful wife. It was decided that he would exile her and embark upon a search for a new wife within the empire.

Suitable candidates first went before a man named Hegai. He counseled the young women on how to conduct themselves in the presence of the king.

A Jew named Mordecai believed that his young cousin Hadassah would make a good queen. She was lovely and had a caring heart and a bright mind. Mordecai had raised Hadassah, that many called Esther, since her parents had died. So it came to pass that Esther was brought also to "Hegai, keeper of the women" (Esther 2:8).

Esther did not reveal she was a Jew. When it was her turn to go in to meet the king, Xerxes fell in love with Esther from the moment he first saw her. He placed upon her head a golden crown and ordered a day of celebration throughout the empire to honor the new royal, Queen Esther.

Mordecai overheard the guards plotting to kill the king and sent word to Esther to warn the monarch. The king ordered the guards be hanged for their treachery against him.

Haman, one of the king's advisors, was the most powerful Persian in the land. Everyone knelt before Haman out of deference . . . everyone, that is, except for Mordecai. Haman, enraged, decided to use his power to kill not only Mordecai but also all Jews in the Persian Empire.

Haman went to the king to outline his case to exterminate the Jews. He told Xerxes that certain people within the kingdom disobeyed the law and exerted an unsavory influence. They should not be tolerated. He convinced the king that his plan had merit and the king gave him a ring with the royal seal. Haman wrote the decree, sealed it in wax, and stamped it. The decree stated that on the thirteenth day of the twelfth month, the people of all the provinces under the rule of the king were to kill all Jews—men, women, and children.

Mordecai put on sackcloth with ashes and went into mourning. He went into the center of the city and cried out bitterly. After her maids told her about Mordecai, Esther sent him new clothes, but he refused to wear them. He begged her to go to the king and plead for mercy for the Jews.

Esther sent a message back to Mordecai. She told him to ask all Jews to pray for her for three days, and then she would go do as he had asked. Three days passed. Esther walked to the king's chamber. He asked her what she wanted. Whatever it was, he would give it to her. She asked the king to join her for a banquet the next night and to invite Haman.

Both men arrived as planned at Esther's sumptuous banquet. Again the king asked Esther what she desired—ask and it would be given. If it please the king, she said, "let my life be given me at my petition, and my people at my request: For we are sold, I and my people, to be destroyed, to be slain, and to perish. But if we had been sold for bondmen and bondwomen, I had held my tongue, although the enemy could not countervail the king's damage" (Esther 7:3–4).

The king, alarmed and enraged, demanded to know the identity of Esther's enemy. Esther told him it was Haman. The king had Haman removed and hanged, then gave Haman's wealth to Esther. He made Mordecai his highest counselor in the land.

EUNICE *(Greek)* Victorious.

EUODIAS *(Greek)* Successful. **NOTABLES:** Euodias and Syntyche were early Christian evangelists and associates of the Apostle Paul (Philippians 4:2).

EUSTACIA *(Latin)* Tranquil.

EVA *(Hebrew)* Life.

EVABELLE *(Hebrew)* Breath of life.

EVE *(Hebrew)* Life. **NOTABLES:** First woman God made, wife of Adam (the first human) and "mother of all living" (Genesis 3:20).

EZRELA *(Hebrew)* God is my strength.

F

FEIGEL *(Hebrew)* Bird.

FIDELITY *(Latin)* Faithful. **VARIATIONS:** Fidelina.

FRAYDA *(Hebrew)* Happy.

G

GADA *(Hebrew)* Lucky.

GAFNA *(Hebrew)* My father rejoices.

GALI *(Hebrew)* Hill; mound; fountain; spring. **VARIATIONS:** Gal, Galice.

GALIA *(Hebrew)* Wave.

GALILEA *(Hebrew)* From Galilee.

GALYA *(Hebrew)* God has redeemed.

GANYA *(Hebrew)* God's garden.

GAVRILLA *(Hebrew)* Heroine.

GAYLE *(Hebrew)* Rejoicing.

GAYORA *(Hebrew)* Valley of light.

GAZIT *(Hebrew)* Smooth stone.

GEFEN *(Hebrew)* Vine.

GELILAH *(Hebrew)* Rolling hills.

GEMMA *(Latin)* Jewel.

GENESIS *(Hebrew)* Beginning. VARIATIONS: Genessa, Genisa, Genisia, Genisis, Jenesis.

GENNELLE *(Hebrew)* God is gracious. VARIATIONS: Gianelle, Janelle.

GEONA *(Hebrew)* Glorification.

GERUSHAH *(Hebrew)* Banishment.

GEVA *(Hebrew)* Hill.

GEVIRAH *(Hebrew)* Queen. VARIATIONS: Gevaryah, Gevaryahu.

GIANA *(Italian)* Feminine form of Gianni or John. VARIATIONS: Geonana, Gia, Gianella, Gianina, Giona.

GIANELLE *(Hebrew)* God is gracious. VARIATIONS: Gianella.

GIBORAH *(Hebrew)* Strong. VARIATIONS: Gibora.

GILA *(Hebrew)* Joy.

GILADAH *(Hebrew)* Hill of testimony.

GILANAH *(Hebrew)* Happy.

GILIAH *(Hebrew)* God's joy.

GINNI *(Latin)* Form of Virgin.

GIOVANNA *(Latin)* God is gracious.

GLORIA *(Latin)* Glory. VARIATIONS: Gloree, Glori, Glorianna, Glorianne, Glorie, Glorielle, Glorria, Glory.

GOMER *(Hebrew)* To finish or complete. NOTABLES: Biblical woman, wife of Hosea, given to sensual pleasure and known for her adultery and harlotry. She bore Hosea two boys named Jezreel and Lo-Ammi and a daughter named Lo-Ruhamah (Hosea 1:1–9).

GRACE *(Latin)* Grace. VARIATIONS: Gracelle, Gracey, Gracia, Graciela, Gracy, Grasiela.

H

HADA *(Hebrew)* Form of Hadassah.

HADAR *(Hebrew)* Splendor; glory.

HADARA *(Hebrew)* Beauty; feminine form of Hadar. VARIATIONS: Hadarah, Haddie.

HADASSAH *(Hebrew)* Myrtle; Hebrew name for Esther. NOTABLES: Esther, wife of King Ahauerus (Esther 2:7).

HADIYA *(Arabic)* Guide. VARIATIONS: Hadi, Hadia.

HAGAR *(Egyptian)* Stranger. NOTABLES: Sarai's Egyptian maidservant who conceived a son, Ishmael, with Sarai's husband, Abram (Genesis 16:1–16, also Genesis 21:9–21). VARIATIONS: Haggar.

Hagar Bears a Child for Sarai and Abram

Abram and Sarai live peacefully with their servants and animals in Canaan for ten years. The Lord had promised to multiply Abram's seed, yet during all those years Abram and Sarai remained childless. Sarai understood that a woman's greatest gift to her husband was to bear heirs. She felt great sadness and fretted over her barrenness. Why had God closed her womb when he had promised that the seed of Abram would be as plentiful as particles of dust? Sarai knew that she was too old to conceive and Abram was even older. Most likely, they would never have a child of their own. Sarai decided they could wait no longer. She approached Abram and told him to go to Hagar, her Egyptian handmaiden, and to lie with her that they might have a child through Hagar. And Abram "went in unto Hagar, and she conceived: and when she saw that she had conceived, her mistress was despised in her eyes" (Genesis 16:4).

Sarai had not expected that Hagar would no longer respect her. Although Sarai had not consulted Hagar about becoming Abram's concubine, she nevertheless rejoiced that there was now to be a child in their home. But Hagar believed that her status in the family was equal to Sarai's now that she would bear the first of Abram's heirs. She treated Sarai as an equal rather than with the respect allotted a mistress. When the relationship with Hagar became unbearable, Sarai went to her husband and told him that the Egyptian girl she had once taken into her heart now despised her. Abram listened thoughtfully to his wife and then assured Sarai that she should deal with Hagar however she thought best.

The two women surely had a confrontation, for Hagar fled into the wilderness. She ran until she came to a fountain on the way to Shur. There she sobbed until an angel of the Lord appeared to her. The angel asked where she was going and why. Hagar explained that she was fleeing from Sarai. "Return to thy mistress," the angel told her, "and submit thyself under her hands." The angel continued, "I will multiply thy seed exceedingly . . . . Behold, thou art with child, and shalt bear a son, and shalt call his name Ishmael; because the Lord hath heard thy affliction" (Genesis 16:9–11). Hagar returned to Abram's tent. She bore him a son and named him Ishmael. Abram was eighty-six.

Ishmael grew and Abram became attached to his son. A quiet truce seemed to prevail between Sarai and Hagar. Years passed. One day God spoke to Abram, telling him that he would be the father of many nations and, likewise, Sarai would be the mother of many nations. God told Abram that from that moment on his name would be Abraham and Sarai would be Sarah.

God gave Abraham a wonderful surprise. He told Abraham, "Sarah thy wife shall bear thee a son indeed; and thou shalt call his name Isaac: and I will establish my covenant with him for an everlasting covenant, and with his seed after him" (Genesis 17:19). If Abraham was not already on his knees in the presence of the Lord, he would have fallen upon them. He laughed and wondered aloud if a one-hundred-year-old man and a ninety-year-old woman could make a baby. God told him that through Sarah, he, the Lord, would establish his nation of people.

Abraham asked God about Ishmael and was told that Hagar's son would be fruitful. In fact, Ishmael would have twelve sons and from them would come a great nation, but it would be through Isaac that God would establish his everlasting covenant with his people, and the sign of that covenant would be circumcision.

Later that day, Abraham called together all the men of his house, including the male servants, for the purpose of circumcising them. "In the selfsame day was Abraham circumcised, and Ishmael his son. And all the men of his house, born in the house, and brought with money of the stranger, were circumcised with him" (Genesis 17:26–27).

HAGGITH *(Hebrew)* Festive; rejoicing.

HAIFA *(Hebrew)* Beautiful beach.

HAMMOLEKETH *(Hebrew)* The queen. NOTABLES: Daughter of Machir and descendant of Gideon. Although she is referenced in the Bible as a mother having descendants, her husband's identity is not revealed (1 Chronicles 7:18).

HAMUTAL *(Hebrew)* Like dew; fresh. **NOTABLES:** Daughter of the Old Testament prophet Jeremiah who married King Josiah.

HANIA *(Hebrew)* Resting place. **VARIATIONS:** Haniya.

HANNAH *(Hebrew)* Grace. **NOTABLES:** The Biblical woman from whom God removed barrenness. She gave birth to four boys and two girls (1 Samuel 1:1–20, 2:21).

HANNI *(Hebrew)* Form of Hannah.

HASNA *(Arabic)* Stone.

HATHOR *(Egyptian)* Goddess of love.

HAVIVA *(Hebrew)* Beloved.

HAZELELPONI *(Hebrew)* The shadow looking on me. **NOTABLES:** Biblical sister of Etam, Jezreel, Ishma, and Idbash (1 Chronicles 4:3).

HEDIAH *(Hebrew)* Echo of God. **VARIATIONS:** Hedia, Hedya.

HELAH *(Greek)* Sun *(Hebrew)* rust. The name of one of Asher's wives (1 Chronicle 4:5).

HEPHZIBA *(Hebrew)* Form of Hephzibah.

HEPHZIBAH *(Hebrew)* My delight is in her; she is my desire. **NOTABLES:** Wife of the King Hezekiah of Judah (2 Kings 21:1).

Hephzibah's husband ruled for twenty-nine years and was the thirteenth king in the succession of the kings of Judah. She gave birth to a son named Manasseh who ruled after his father. When Manasseh assumed the throne, he was a mere twelve-year-old and he ruled for fifty-five years. Depending on which passage of the Bible you read, he was either a wicked king—perhaps the most wicked to ever rule Judah—or a monarch who repented his wickedness, sought God's forgiveness, and received divine mercy (2 Kings 21:1–18; 2 Chronicles 33:1–20). He asks the Lord for mercy in the Prayer of Manasseh, excluded from the Bible but found in the Apocrypha (scriptural texts of questionable authorship or authenticity). Hephzibah, therefore, spent the greater part of her lifetime as queen, queen-mother of Manasseh, or queen-grandmother of Amon.

During her husband's nearly thirty-year reign, Hephzibah would have been at Hezekiah's side during the destruction of Judah by Sennacherib, who at that time was the king of Assyria (2 Kings 18:13–14). Archeological evidence in the form of broken storage jar handles unearthed in modern Israel confirmed the reign of Hezekiah. The Bible states that in the fourteenth year of Hezekiah's rule, Sennacherib went on a rampage, tyrannizing the fortified cities of Judah. He captured many of them, prompting Hezekiah to send the warring king a message that he would pay any amount to get the Assyrians out of Judah. After he paid vast sums of silver and gold, robbing the temple of Jerusalem to do so, an angel of death took the lives of 185,000 of Senn before they could take the city of Jerusalem.

Modern sources assert that Hezekiah was a fair king, respected by his subjects in the southern kingdom of Judah. Perhaps Hephzibah quietly stood by her husband when he was faced with the seemingly insurmountable odds of losing his kingdom to Sennecherib. It would have meant certain slavery for his people. The massive army of the Assyrians threatened the gates of his capital city, Jerusalem. They shouted to his people to abandon their loyalty to him. They ridiculed the God of the Hebrews. It must have been a daunting period and terrible circumstance for Hezikiah to face. His advisors would have given him their input, but it may have been his wife whose soft and gentle presence and faith in the Lord turned his thoughts to prayer in that time of crisis. "Then Isaiah the son of Amoz sent to Hezekiah, saying, "Thus saith the Lord God of Israel, That which thou hast prayed to me against Sennacherib king of Assyria I have heard"" (2 Kings 19:20).

Hephzibah's son Manasseh, according to some sources, may have co-ruled for a period of time with his father. When his father died, Hephzibah would have felt the pain of all religious mothers when their children rebel against the faith. Her son did abominations against the God of Israel and the work, practices, and policies of his father. He surrounded himself with magicians, wizards, and those known for conjuring dead spirits. The Bible states that her son did much evil (2 Kings 21:1–9). Not much else is known about the woman whose name means "my delight is in her." But her name was important because God said he would remove "Forsaken" as a name for his people and call them by a new name. "Thou shalt no more be termed Forsaken; neither shall thy land any more be termed Desolate: but thou shalt be called Hephzibah, and thy land Beulah: for the Lord delighteth in thee, and thy land shall be married" (Isaiah 62:4).

HEPSIE *(Hebrew)* Form of Hephzibah.

HERODIAS *(Hebrew)* Feminine form of Herod. NOTABLES: The woman married to Philip, brother of the Roman tetrarch Herod. She persuaded her daughter Salome to ask Herod for the head of John the Baptist (Matthew 14:3–12; Mark 6:17–29; Luke 3:19–20).

HODESH *(Hebrew)* New moon.

HODIAH *(Hebrew)* The praise of the Lord. NOTABLES: Wife of Asher who was also the sister of Naham (1 Chronicles 4:19).

HOGLAH *(Hebrew)* Quail. NOTABLES: One of the five daughters of Zelophehad (Numbers 26:33, 27:1).

HOSANNA *(Hebrew)* Rescue us.

HULDAH *(Hebrew)* Loved one. NOTABLES: The prophetess wife of Shallum who was consulted by Josiah, king of Judah (2 Kings 22:14).

I

IDRA *(Hebrew)* Fig tree.

IKIA *(Hebrew)* God helps me.

ILANA *(Hebrew)* Tree. VARIATIONS: Elana, Elanit, Ileana.

ILANIT *(Hebrew)* Feminine form of Ilan; tree.

ISHA *(Hebrew)* Woman.

ISMAELA *(Hebrew)* God listens. VARIATIONS: Isma, Mael, Maella.

ITIAH *(Hebrew)* God is here.

IVRIA *(Hebrew)* From Abraham's land.

IYANA *(Hebrew)* Feminine form of John. VARIATIONS: Iyania, Iyanna, Iyannia.

IYRIA *(Hebrew)* In the land of Abraham.

J

JACINDA *(Greek)* Beautiful. VARIATIONS: Jacinta.

JACINTHE *(Greek)* Hyacinth. VARIATIONS: Jakinda.

JACOBINA *(Hebrew)* Supplanter; feminine form of Jacob.

JAEL *(Hebrew)* To ascend. The woman who nailed a tent peg into the head of Sisera, the military commander fighting against the Israelites (Judges 4:17–22). VARIATIONS: Yael.

JAEN *(Hebrew)* Ostrich.

JAFFA *(Hebrew)* Beautiful.

JAFFE *(Hebrew)* Form of Jaffa; beautiful.

JAMEE *(Hebrew)* Supplanter. VARIATIONS: Jamie, Jaymee.

JAMIE *(Hebrew)* Form of Jamee; feminine form of James.

JAN *(Hebrew)* God is good.

JANAE *(Hebrew)* God answers.

JANNA *(Hebrew)* Short form of Johanna, a derivative of the masculine John or Johann.

JANOAH *(Hebrew)* Quiet.

JARON *(Hebrew)* To shout; to sing. VARIATIONS: Yaron.

JECHOLIAH *(Hebrew)* Strong in Jehovah. NOTABLES: Wife of Amaziah, the king of Judah, and mother of Azariah (2 Kings 15:2).

JEDIDAH *(Hebrew)* Beloved of God. NOTABLES: Mother of Josiah (2 Kings 21:1).

JEHOADDAN *(Hebrew)* One Jehovah adorns. NOTABLES: Queen to King Joash and mother of Amaziah (2 Kings 14:1–2).

JEHOSHABEATH *(Hebrew)* Daughter of Jehoram. NOTABLES: The daughter of a king and the wife of a priest (Jehoiada) who hid young prince Joash from Athaliah, the prince's grandmother and Jehosheba's own sister. Athaliah wished to kill him and his brothers because he was in line to succeed his recently deceased father to the throne and Athaliah wanted to reign as queen of Judah (2 Chronicles 22:11). VARIATIONS: Jehosheba.

JEHUDIJAH *(Hebrew)* Praise of the Lord. NOTABLES: Mother of Jered (1 Chronicles 4:18).

JEMIMA *(Hebrew)* Dove. NOTABLES: Eldest daughter of Job (Job 42:12–14).

Jemima, Job's First-Born Daughter Following His Travails

Job suffered a reversal of fortune when God allowed Satan to test Job's piety. God told Satan he could do whatever he wanted except take Job's life. Job lost his ten children, his livestock (7,000 sheep, 3,000 camels, 500 oxen, and 500 donkeys), his prosperous household, and his health, but his faith in God never wavered. Job even prayed for his two friends who had told him to renounce the Lord. The Lord showed Job mercy and Job's life began anew. His prosperity returned even greater than it had been before his afflictions. He and his wife came together again, and he had seven sons and three daughters. The first-born girl was named Jemima; and the name of the second was Kezia; and the name of third was Keren-Happuch. "And in all the land were no women found so fair as the daughters of Job: and their father gave them inheritance among their brethren" (Job 42:15).

JEMINA *(Hebrew)* Right-handed.

JEREMIA *(Hebrew)* The Lord is great; feminine form of Jeremiah.

JERIOTH *(Hebrew)* Kettles; to break apart. NOTABLES: Possibly a wife or concubine of Caleb, son of

Hezron, with whom he had children (1 Chronicles 2:18).

JERUSHA *(Hebrew)* Possession; inheritance. **NOTABLES:** Daughter of Zadok and queen mother of Jotham, the heir to Uzziah, king of Judah (2 Kings 15:32–33).

JESSICA *(Hebrew)* He beholds.

JETHRA *(Hebrew)* Plenty.

JEZEBEL *(Hebrew)* Unexalted. **NOTABLES:** Wife of King Ahab. Her deeds were so wicked that her servants threw her from the palace window and dogs ate her (2 Kings 9:30–37).

JOAN *(Latin)* God's gracious gift. **NOTABLES:** Jean d'Arc (St. Joan of Arc).

JOANNA *(Latin)* God is gracious. **NOTABLES:** A follower of Jesus who was the wife of Herod's steward Chuza (Luke 8:2–3).

JOBY *(Hebrew)* Persecuted.

JOCHEBED *(Hebrew)* God is our glory. **NOTABLES:** Mother of Miriam, Aaron, and Moses who gave up Moses to be raised by Pharaoh's daughter (Exodus 2:1–10, 6:20; Numbers 26:59).

JODY *(Hebrew)* Praised.

JOELLE *(Hebrew)* Jehovah is willing.

JONATHA *(Hebrew)* Gift of God; feminine form of Jonathan.

JONINA *(Hebrew)* Dove.

JORA *(Hebrew)* Autumn rain. VARIATIONS: Jorah.

JORI *(Hebrew)* Form of Jordan; short form of Marjorie. Variations, Joree, Jorie, Jorri, Jory.

JOSEPHINE *(Hebrew)* God will increase. VARIATIONS: Josee, Josefa, Josefina, Josefine, Josepha, Josephe, Josephene, Josephina, Josetta, Josette, Josey, Josi, Josie.

JUBILEE *(Hebrew)* Jubilant.

JUDAH *(Hebrew)* To praise; anglicized form of Yehuda. NOTABLES: Jesus was from the tribe of Judah.

JUDITH *(Hebrew)* Admired; praised. NOTABLES: The Jewess who got the enemy military leader Holofernes drunk and then cut off his head (Judith 13:1–9). VARIATIONS: Judey, Judi, Judie, Judita, Judite, Juditha, Judy, Judye.

JULIA *(Latin)* Young. VARIATIONS: Julee, Juli, Juliana, Juliane, Julianna, Juliette.

JUNE *(Latin)* Moon.

JUNIA *(Latin)* Youthful. NOTABLES: The Christian woman who, with her husband Andronicus, was called "of note among the Apostles" by the Apostle Paul (Romans 16:7). The declaration by Paul has been used by some feminist Christians to suggest that women during the Apostolic Age might have served as apostles. VARIATIONS: Iounias.

JUNO *(Latin)* Queen of heaven. NOTABLES: The moniker "Queen of Heaven" has often been applied to

Mary, mother of Jesus as well as to the Roman goddess Juno and the Greek goddess Hera.

JUSTINE *(Hebrew/Latin)* Just and true.

K

KALINIT *(Hebrew)* Anemone. NOTABLES: A flower indigenous to the Mediterranean area.

KANAH *(Hebrew)* Of reeds. VARIATIONS: Cana, Canah, Cannah, Kana, Kaneh, Kanika.

KARMA *(Hebrew)* Orchard *(Hindi)* fate, destiny. VARIATIONS: Carma.

KARMELLE *(Hebrew)* Fruitful orchard. VARIATIONS: Karmell.

KARMIA *(Hebrew)* Lord's vineyard.

KATHERINE *(Greek)* Pure; virginal. VARIATIONS: Caitriona, Caren, Caron, Caryn, Caye, Kaethe, Kai, Kaila, Kaitlin, Karen, Karena, Karin, Karina, Karine, Karon, Karrin, Karyn, Karyna, Karynn, Kata, Kataleen, Katalin, Katalina, Kateke, Katerina, Katerinka, Katharin, Katharina, Katharine, Katie, Katrine, Katy.

KATRIEL *(Hebrew)* Crowned by God.

KEDEMOTH *(Hebrew)* Antiquity; old age. NOTABLES: Name of a city north of the Arnon River in a region occupied by the Tribe of Reuben, one of the twelve tribes of Israel (Joshua 13:15–18).

KELILAH *(Hebrew)* Victorious; crown of laurel. VARIATIONS: Kaille, Kalia, Kayle, Keila, Keilah, Kelila, Kellila, Kellula, Kyle, Kylia.

KELULA *(Yiddish)* Girlfriend.

KEREN *(Hebrew)* Horn.

KETIFA *(Hebrew)* To pick. VARIATIONS: Ketipha.

KETINA *(Hebrew)* Girl.

KETURAH *(Hebrew)* Incense; perfume. NOTABLES: Wife of the Hebrew patriarch Abraham (Genesis 25: 1–4).

KEZAH *(Hebrew)* Cassiah plant. NOTABLES: Job's second daughter born after Job's many travails (Job 42:14). Her sisters' names were Jemima and Keren-Happuch. VARIATIONS: Keziah.

KIRIAH *(Hebrew)* Village. VARIATIONS: Kira, Kiria, Kyria.

KITRA *(Hebrew)* Wreath.

L

LAEL *(Hebrew)* From God.

LAILAH *(Arabic)* Sweetheart; born at night. VARIATIONS: Laila, Lailaa, Lalee, Laliah, Layla, Leyla.

LAODICE *(Uncertain origin, possibly Greek or Syrian)* Just people. NOTABLES: Divorced first wife of Antiochus II who murdered Bernice and Bernice's son after the monarch Antiochus died and before Ptolemy

III could ascend the throne. The murderous act precipitated a new Syrian war.

LARETTA *(Latin)* Sweet laurel tree; honor; victory. VARIATIONS: Lara, Laurie, Loretta.

LAURA *(Latin)* Laurel. VARIATIONS: Lauraine, Laural, Laureine, Laurilee, Laurinda.

LEAH *(Hebrew)* Weary. NOTABLES: Daughter of Laban who married Jacob through her father's trickery after Jacob had worked seven years for Laban in order to marry Rachel. Her sister Rachel also married Jacob. He had to earn the right to marry her all over again and worked another seven years for Laban (Genesis 29:23–30).

LEDAH *(Hebrew)* Birth. VARIATIONS: Leda, Leta.

LEHABIM *(Hebrew)* Flaming; inflamed; swords. NOTABLES: One of Noah's descendants born after the flood. Although the name commonly appears as a male one, some sources list it as female (Genesis 10:13).

LEMUELA *(Hebrew)* Devoted to God; feminine version of Lemuel. VARIATIONS: Lemuella.

LEVANA *(Hebrew)* White moon. VARIATIONS: Livana.

LEVIA *(Hebrew)* Join together or combine forces.

LIAT *(Hebrew)* You are mine.

LIOR *(Hebrew)* My light.

LISBETH *(Hebrew)* Form of Elizabeth.

LO-RUHAMAH *(Hebrew)* Not loved; no mercy. NOTABLES: Daughter born to Gomer and Hosea (Hosea 1:6).

LUCINDA *(Latin)* Beautiful light.

LUCY *(Latin)* Form of Lucinda.

LYDIA *(Greek)* A woman from Lydia. NOTABLES: In the Acts of the Apostles, Lydia was a business-woman, a dyer of purple cloth, who invited the Apostle Paul to be her houseguest in the city of Thyatira, a region of Greece (Acts 16:14–15, 40).

M

MAACHAH *(Egyptian/Hebrew)* Kneel; may be a short form of Michaiah. NOTABLES: Daughter of Uriel and Gibeah (2 Chronicles 13:2) possibly daughter of Absalom (2 Chronicles 11:20).

MAGDALENE *(Hebrew)* Woman from Magdala. NOTABLES: Mary Magdalene, follower, friend, and confidante of Jesus who is mentioned in all four of the New Testament gospels as an eyewitness to his resurrection (Matthew 28:1–8; Mark 16:9; Luke 24:10; John 20:1–17). VARIATIONS: Mada, Madalena, Madeleine, Madelina, Madeline, Madelyn, Madge, Madilin, Madilyn, Madolyn, Magda, Maggada.

Mary Magdalene, Eyewitness to the Risen Jesus

Mary Magdalene is one of the most recognized names in the Bible. Although the church long miscast her as the Bible's most repentant prostitute, biblical scholars say there has never been any proof to support that assertion. Mary Magdalene's profile has benefited from numerous books in popular culture, perhaps the most successful being *The Da Vinci Code*, which alluded to a cover-up by the church of a possible marriage between Mary Magdalene and Jesus, an assertion that many Christians consider to be false.

In the New Testament, Mary Magdalene's name appears fourteen times. The number of times her name appears may suggest her level of importance in the community of Jesus followers during her lifetime. All four of the gospel accounts mention Mary Magdalene in conjunction with the risen Jesus. Since the Resurrection is central to the Christian religion, her eyewitness account makes her a prominent figure in Christian tradition.

She was the woman from Magdala. In Palestine during Jesus' lifetime, Magdala was located on the shore of Lake Gennesaret (also called the Sea of Tiberias by the Romans). The place stood between the cities of Capernaum and Tiberias. Jesus traveled through that region (Matthew 15:39). The place appears in the writings of Josephus, a first-century Jewish historian.

Mary Magdalene has also been called Miriham, Miriam, Mariamme, and Miryam (means "bitter"). Perhaps Jesus and Mary Magdalene's paths crossed when he preached in or near Magdala. The Gospel of Luke states that many women had evil spirits and infirmities cast out by Jesus. In Mary Magdalene's case, Jesus exorcised seven devils from her (Luke 8:2; Mark 16:9).

Some modern speculations suggest that she may have been older than Jesus and also have had some means to support herself (perhaps she was a widow), because her name is associated with a place name rather than a man's name, which would have been more customary.

The Gnostic Gospels are gospels excluded from the books of the Bible. One Gnostic Gospel is named The Gospel of Mary [Magdalene]. She is the only woman to have a gospel named for her. That text portrays Mary Magdalene as a close friend and confidante of Jesus and also an astute student who learned quickly and excelled in questioning him about theology.

Certain biblical scholars and feminist theologians have suggested that Mary Magdalene was a female leader who held the Jesus followers and disciples together following the death of their leader. She may have had her own disciples. Certainly the male Apostles did.

Mary stood vigil at the foot of Jesus' cross along with his mother and other women. When they took down his body, it was taken to the garden of Joseph of Arimathea. The women, including Mary Magdalene, wanted to prepare the body for burial in the custom of the Jews, but the arrival of the Sabbath prevented them from finishing their work.

It was Sunday morning before she could race back to the tomb (Matthew 28:1; Mark 16:1), and then she found it empty (Matthew 28:5–6). She hurried to tell Peter and John (John 20:1–2), who went to see for themselves.

Biblical scholars assert that the fact that Mary Magdalene was the pre-eminent witness to the risen Jesus adds weight to the historicity of the event, because the

Law did not accept the testimony of women. Mark 16:9 states that Jesus appeared "first to Mary Magdalene." The Gospel of Matthew states that she was with the *other Mary* (Matthew 28:1). The Gospel of Luke makes reference to several women, including Mary Magdalene and Jesus' mother. The two of them saw two men in shining garments who told them that Jesus "is risen" (Luke 24:1–10). Finally, John 20:10–17 states that Mary Magdalene met Christ alone in the garden.

She is referred to as Apostle to the Apostles in Catholicism, and in other traditions, she is referred to as the Thirteenth Apostle, and The Woman Who Knew the All. In the Catholic and eastern churches, her feast day is observed on July 22.

MAGDIEL *(Hebrew)* Fruit chosen by God; preciousness. NOTABLES: Place name, possibly an Edomite province where descendants of Esau, brother of Jacob, settled (Genesis 36:43).

MAHALAH *(Hebrew)* Affection; tenderness. VARIATIONS: Mahalia, Mahaliah, Mahalla, Mahelia, Mehalia.

MAHALATH *(Hebrew)* Lyre, lute. NOTABLES: Daughter of Ishmael. Ishmael was born of Hagar, concubine/wife of Abraham (Genesis 28:9).

MALKAH *(Hebrew)* Queen. VARIATIONS: Malkia, Malkiah, Malkie.

MANGENA *(Hebrew)* Song.

MARA *(Hebrew)* Bitter; form of Maria. NOTABLES: The widowed Naomi changed her name to Mara after the death her husband and her two boys (Ruth 1:20). VARIATIONS: Marah.

MARCELLA *(Latin)* Martial.

MARIA *(Hebrew)* Bitter; sea of bitterness; form of Mary.

MARIAH *(Egyptian)* God is my teacher; form of Mary.

MARNI *(Hebrew)* To rejoice.

MARTHA *(Arabic)* Lady. NOTABLES: A dutiful and practical friend of Jesus. Her sister was named Mary and her brother was Lazarus (Luke 10:38–42; John 11:1, 12:2)

Martha, the Dutiful Sister

Martha was the dutiful one whereas her sister Mary seemed to be more introspective and spiritually inclined. They were sisters of Lazarus, followers of Jesus; they lived in a small house in Bethany near Jerusalem.

On one occasion when Jesus visited them, Martha busily toiled in the kitchen to prepare a meal for their guests while Mary was content to sit near the feet of Jesus while he talked. Martha became annoyed that her sister was doing nothing while she slaved away to prepare the food. Finally, she went to Jesus and complained, "Lord, dost thou not care that my sister hath left me to serve alone? Bid her therefore that she help me." And Jesus answered and said unto her, "Martha, Martha, thou art careful and troubled about many things: But one thing is needful: and Mary hath chosen that good part, which shall not be taken away from her" (Luke 10:40–42).

Jesus patiently pointed out to Martha that while she worried about all manner of things in this world, Mary had chosen to learn about things not of this world but the world of the heavenly Father. In contrast to Martha fussing over food, Mary sought nourishment for her soul. Jesus said that the "good part" would not ever be taken from her (Luke 10:42).

MARTHE *(Hebrew)* Bitter.

MARY *(Hebrew)* Beloved. NOTABLES: Mary, mother of Jesus (Matthew 2:11; Luke 1:27); Mary Magdalene, pre-eminent female disciple of Jesus and eyewitness to the risen Jesus (John 19:25, 20:1–18); Mary of Bethany, sister of Martha and Lazarus and anointer of Jesus (Matthew 26:6–13; John 11:1–2, 12:1–8); Mary, wife of Cleophas (John 19:25); Mary, mother of James and Joses (Matthew 27:55–56, 61; Mark 15:40–41). VARIATIONS: Maaria, Maartje, Maija, Mair, Maire, Maja, Malaea, Malia, Maree, Mariah, Maribel, Maribella, Mariska, Marissa, Mayra, Meriel, Merrilee, Merry, Mia, Mimi, Minnie, Miriam, Miriamne, Mitzi, Moira, Moire.

Mary, the Mother of Jesus

Mary was born of Ann and Joachim, a pious Jewish couple who obeyed the Laws given to the Hebrews through Moses. Little is known about Mary's early life. Most likely, her parents were unable to conceive. According to tradition, her father, Joachim, married Ann when he was forty-nine and she was twenty. Their community viewed their barrenness as a punishment from the Lord, and the couple felt ostracized. Joachim even tried to give his annual tithe to the temple and was turned away because he was sterile (thus cursed in the eyes of his fellow Jews) and not welcome to stand with them, men who were able to father sons.

One day, as Ann prayed in their home for a child, Joachim went into the desert to pray. An angel suddenly appeared and told him that his wife was carrying a child filled with the Holy Spirit. The angel instructed him to name the child Mary and to honor their promise to God to send the child when she was weaned to the temple where she would serve the Lord.

As Mary grew up in the temple, she would have learned about her Jewish roots and about God and his commandments. Her earliest appearances in the Bible are in the New Testament gospels of Matthew and Luke. She is a young virgin who is visited by the angel Gabriel and told that God was about to bless her among women. Through the Holy Spirit, she would conceive a child. Mary was alarmed. She was betrothed to Joseph but not yet married. The angel assuaged her fears. And Mary, ever obedient to God's will in her life, said, "Behold the handmaid of the Lord; be it unto me according to thy word. And the angel departed from her" (Luke 1:38).

Mary and Joseph traveled from Nazareth to Bethlehem (Joseph's ancestral town, for he was of the house and lineage of David) when she was about to deliver. They were compelled to do so in order to give census information for tax purposes (Luke 2:1). People were on the move and the inns were full. Mary delivered her child, wrapped him in swaddling clothes, and laid him in a manger (Luke 2:7). After eight days, Mary and Joseph took their young son to the temple for the naming ceremony and to have him circumcised. Simeon, an old man filled with the Holy Spirit, saw the child and recognized him as the "Lord's Christ" (Luke 2:26–33).

When Jesus was twelve years old, the family made a trip to Jerusalem for Passover. On the return trip home, Mary was quite disturbed to find her son missing. They retraced their steps back into the city and found Jesus discoursing in the temple with the learned priests. Mary asked him, "Son, why hast thou thus dealt with us? Behold, thy father and I have sought thee sorrowing." And he said unto them, "How is it that ye sought me? Wist ye not that I must be about my Father's business?" (Luke 2:48–49).

Jesus, the Bible states, grew in stature and in favor with God and man. His cousin John, the Baptist, a man of great spiritual conviction and charisma, called upon all Jews to repent and serve God. He baptized Jesus, and Jesus went on to preach throughout the land. He taught people many truths and gave signs of the miraculous power of God at work when he healed the sick and raised the dead. The Bible does not say that Mary was ever baptized, but she was often by his side on his travels during his ministry. She undoubtedly was in Jerusalem for the last Passover. She stood vigil at the cross where Jesus was crucified. With her were Mary Magdalene; Mary, mother of James and Joses; and the mother of Zebedee's children (Matthew 27:56).

There is only speculation and traditional stories to offer insight into Mary's life after Jesus' death. From the cross, her son entrusted her to the care of the disciple he loved. Some sources assert that she went to Ephesus with John, the Beloved Disciple. Other traditions say she went to the southern part of Gaul (France), and oral stories there are strong and have survived for centuries.

The mother of Jesus is known by many titles: The Virgin Mary, The Blessed Virgin, Mother of God, Mother of All Living, The Immaculate Conception, Our Lady, Theotokos (in the eastern Orthodox and related churches), Co-Redemptrix, God Bearer, Our Lady of Sorrows, Our Lady of Prompt Succor, Our Lady of Perpetual Help, Our Lady of Lourdes, and Our Lady of Guadalupe, among them. Because she was without sin and bore the Son of God, Jesus of Nazareth, whom Christians regard as the Savior of humankind, Mary has always been regarded as blessed and worthy of veneration.

MATTHEA *(Hebrew)* Gift from God; feminine form of Matthias. VARIATIONS: Mattea, Matteya.

MAYIM *(Hebrew)* Water.

MEARAH *(Hebrew)* Den; cave; emptying out. VARIATIONS: Meara, Meera, Mira.

MEHETABEL *(Hebrew)* God's favor. VARIATIONS: Mehitabel.

MERAB *(Hebrew)* Abundant. NOTABLES: Daughter of Saul who was supposed to have been given to David but instead was given to Adriel the Meholathite as a wife (1 Samuel 14:49, 18:19).

MESHULLEMETH *(Hebrew)* Female friend. NOTA-BLES: Daughter of Haruz of Jotbah and wife of Manasseh. She bore Manasseh a son named Amon, who became king of Judah at twenty-two after his father died (2 Kings 21:19–20).

MICHAELA *(Hebrew)* Who is like God; feminine form of Michael; form of Michal.

MICHAIAH *(Hebrew)* Who is like God, kneel; form of Maacah. NOTABLES: Queen and mother of Abijah (2 Chronicles 13:1–2).

MICHAL *(Hebrew)* Brook. NOTABLES: King Saul's daughter and David's first wife. She opposed her father (1 Samuel 14:49, 18:20–29, 19:17).

Michal, Married and Reclaimed by David

Michal was the daughter of King Saul. He had three sons, Jonathon, Ishvi, and Malchishua. His two daughters were Merab and Michal (1 Samuel 14:49). Saul told David that he would give his daughter Merab to him as a wife. David wondered why he, of modest means and lineage, should be so lucky as to become son-in-law to a king. But Saul did not keep his word. When it came time to give Merab to David, she "was given unto Adriel the Meholathite to wife" (1 Samuel 18:19).

Saul feared David and was jealous of him. David had beaten Goliath, an accomplishment that brought women out of all the cities of Israel rejoicing and proclaiming that while Saul had slain thousands, David had slain tens of thousands. David was young, virile, and popular. Saul told his servants to commune with David and tell him that the king delighted in him and that he would indeed become the king's son-in-law. When David had been softened up with praise, Saul told his servants to relay to David that that he need not worry about paying a bride price. Instead he should simply bring the king 100 foreskins from Philistines warriors. In other words, David should risk his life to kill some of the king's enemies. Saul had hoped that David would fall by the hand of the Philistines. But David and his men did as requested and brought back the Philistine foreskins.

Saul gave his daughter Michal to David and feared David more than ever. He even told Jonathan and his servants to kill his new son-in-law. But Jonathan and his sister Michal both loved David and on separate occasions warned him of Saul's enmity. Whether or not David ever consummated his marriage with Michal or even returned her love remains a question. They never had any children. He spent a great deal of time away from her fighting in battles. In fact, David spent more time in the company of Saul's son than with Michal, and he seemed to have rejected his relationship with her.

Saul eventually married her off to someone else, a man named Phaltiel, a man of Saul's own tribe of Benjamin. Saul reasoned that with Michal married to Phaltiel, his former son-in-law could no longer make any claim to the throne. Once again, Saul showed a ruthless side. His daughters were like pawns to be used in his political strategies. In an effort to unite the northern kingdom of Israel with the southern kingdom of Judah, David reclaimed Michal from Phaltiel (2 Samuel 3:13–16). She epitomized royal grace and dignity and even complained about David's behavior when he danced in a vulgar manner in the street as the Ark of the Covenant was brought into Jerusalem (2 Samuel 6:16–23).

MILCAH *(Hebrew)* Queen. NOTABLES: Hebrew woman who was the wife of Nahor (brother of the Jewish patriarch Abraham) and mother of Bethuel. She was also the daughter of Haran; they lived in ancient Mesopotamia (Genesis 11:29, 24:24).

MIRIAM *(Hebrew)* To rebel; bitterness. NOTABLES: Biblical woman who spoke against her brother Moses, leader of the ancient Hebrews, and was stricken with leprosy (Numbers 12:1–10); sister of Moses and Aaron who watched over baby Moses and enlisted Pharaoh's daughter to get Moses' birth mother to wet-nurse him (Exodus 2:3–10). VARIATIONS: Miryam, Myriam.

N

NAAMAH *(Hebrew)* Pleasantness; comforted by God.

NAOMI *(Hebrew)* My delight; my sweet. NOTABLES: The woman who, after the death of her sons, returned to Bethlehem with her daughter-in-law Ruth and changed her name to Mara, meaning "bitter" (Ruth 1:1–22).

NAPIA *(Latin)* Nymph.

NASEEMA *(Arabic)* Zephyr.

NASREEN *(Arabic)* Jonquil. VARIATIONS: Nasrin.

NASYA *(Hebrew)* God's miracle.

NATALA *(Latin)* Born on Christmas. VARIATIONS: Natalie, Natalii, Nathalee, Nathalie.

NATANIAH *(Hebrew)* That which God has given; God's gift. VARIATIONS: Netania, Netanya, Nethaniah.

NEDAVIAH *(Hebrew)* God is charitable. VARIATIONS: Nedavia, Nedavya, Nediva.

NEHUSHTA *(Hebrew)* Uncertain. NOTABLES: Daughter of Elnathan, and wife of Jehoiakim and mother of Jehoiachin, Kings of Judah (2 Kings 24:8, 12, 15).

NEMERA *(Hebrew)* Leopard.

NERA *(Hebrew)* Candlelight.

NERIDA *(Greek)* Sea nymph.

NEVIAH *(Hebrew)* Seer.

NOGA *(Hebrew)* Morning light.

NURA *(Aramaic)* Light. VARIATIONS: Noor, Noura, Nurah, Nuri.

NURITA *(Hebrew)* Flowering plant.

NYMPHA *(Greek)* Goddess. NOTABLES: Christian woman who was a helper of the Apostle Paul (Colossians 4:15).

O

OBEDIENCE *(Latin)* To listen or to hear.

ODEDA *(Hebrew)* Powerful.

ODERA *(Hebrew)* Plow.

ODIYA *(Hebrew)* Song of the Lord.

OFIRA *(Hebrew)* Gold.

OMA *(Hebrew)* Devout.

OPHIRA *(Hebrew)* Gold.

ORIT *(Hebrew)* Light.

ORLI *(Hebrew)* My light. VARIATIONS: Orly.

ORPAH *(Hebrew)* Forelock, fawn, gazelle, back of the neck. NOTABLES: Moabitess who was the widowed daughter-in-law of Naomi and who accompanied Naomi part of the way back to Bethlehem before returning to Moab (Ruth 1:14).

OZARA *(Hebrew)* Treasure.

P

PAULA *(Latin)* Small. VARIATIONS: Paola, Paolina, Pauleen, Paulene, Pauletta, Paulette, Paulina, Pauline.

PAZIA *(Hebrew)* Golden.

PELAGIA *(Greek)* Sea.

PENINNAH *(Hebrew)* Jewel. NOTABLES: Peninnah was one of Elkanah's two wives; the other was Hannah. Peninnah bore Elkanah children and taunted Hannah for being barren (1 Samuel 1:2).

Elkanah from Ramathaim had two wives, Peninnah and Hannah. He loved Hannah first and longed to have children with her, but God had closed her womb. Men in biblical times had to have heirs, so Elkanah took Peninnah for a wife as well. Being a pious man with a strong faith that God would one day bless Hannah with babies, Elkanah went up to the temple at Shiloh each year to offer his sacrifice to the Lord along with his prayers for his barren wife. Peninnah looked upon the outing as an occasion to chastise Hannah for being unable to have children. Surely she had done something to offend God. Her mean-spirit-edness often caused Hannah to break down in tears and refuse to eat. Elkanah would offer his weeping wife a double portion of food, but Hannah would not accept it.

Privately, Hannah promised God that if given a son, she would consecrate the child to do the Lord's work his entire life. But Hannah remained barren and Peninnah continued to have babies.

Elkanah was distressed. One day he asked if he were not better than ten sons. It was his way of showing his deep love and affection for Hannah. He gave her gifts and showed her love through his tender affection and steadfast loyalty. Such favoritism caused Peninnah to step up her criticism of her sister wife.

One day, God heard Hannah's prayer and gave her the son she had wanted for so long. Elkanah and Hannah were ecstatic. They named their son Samuel. When he was weaned, they took their child to Shiloh and gave him over to the care of Eli, the priest. Eli would raise Samuel in the temple. He would do the Lord's work for the rest of his life. But that did not mean that his father Elkanah, his mother Hannah, or the siblings that Peninnah had produced with his father would forget him. There was always the annual trek up to Shiloh to offer prayers and a sacrifice to the Lord.

Hannah kept her promise to God. And every year, after that, she made a new coat for Samuel and took it to him at Shiloh. Eli also prayed for Hannah and Elkanah to have other children. God heard Eli's prayers as well, and Elkanah and Hannah were blessed with several other offspring.

Perhaps Peninnah came to understand that God could open a woman's womb just as well as close it and that her husband might have been as loving to her as he was to Hannah if only she could learn to be less critical and more loving and supportive.

PERACH *(Hebrew)* Blossom.

PERSIS *(Greek)* Woman from Persia.

PHEBE *(Greek)* Light. NOTABLES: An early Christian woman who served as a deaconess of the church at Cenchrea and was a friend of the Apostle Paul (Romans 16:1). VARIATION: Phoebe.

PRIELA *(Hebrew)* Fruit of the Lord.

PRISCA *(Latin)* Form of Priscilla.

PRISCILLA *(Latin)* Old. NOTABLES: An early Christian woman who, with her husband Aquila, was mentioned in a letter to the Romans written by the Apostle Paul (Romans 16:1–3).

PRISSY *(Latin)* Short form of Priscilla.

PRUDENCE *(Latin)* Cautiousness.

PSYCHE *(Greek)* Soul.

PUAH *(Hebrew)* Splendid. NOTABLES: One of two midwives who refused to obey Pharaoh's order to kill infant Jewish boys (Exodus 1:15–22).

Puah and Shifra Defy Pharaoh's Order

These two midwives knew the explicit order from Pharaoh was to kill all newborn Jewish boys. The Egyptian king feared that the burgeoning Hebrew population would threaten the security of Egypt. But the Bible states that Puah and Shifra feared God and refused to obey Pharaoh's command. As midwives, they were trained to provide support to women in labor and to protect and help the infant emerge from its mother's womb into the world. Rather than telling Pharaoh that they refused to murder the infants, an act that would have meant death for the two of them and certainly the death of countless Jewish male babies, the two midwives figured out another approach. They simply didn't do it.

When Pharaoh called them in and asked them to account for their disobedience, the two women replied that they didn't kill the boys "Because the Hebrew women are not as the Egyptian women; for they are lively, and are delivered ere the midwives come in unto them" (Exodus 1:19). In other words, the Hebrew women were almost like animals that could birth their young without help from others. They only called for midwives when they were finished and had their babies in their arms. Pharaoh must have believed them and left them alone after that, because the Bible says that God was pleased with Puah and Shifra and he made them houses (Exodus 1:20–21). Puah and Shifra became known as heroines among the Hebrews.

Q

QUEEN *(Latin)* Title of rank that is sometimes used as a name. NOTABLES: Queen mother in Hebrew was *gebirah*. Ashtoreth was called "Queen of Heaven" (Jeremiah 7:18), a title also used for the Egyptian goddess Isis, the Sumerian goddess Ianna, and Mary, the mother of Jesus. Other queens and queen mothers included Candace of Ethiopia (Acts 8:27); Esther (Esther 1:17); Maacah (1 Kings 15:13–14); Sheba (1 Kings 10:1; 2 Chronicles 9:1–12); Tahpenes, Pharaoh's sister and wife of Hadad (1 Kings 11:19–20); and Vashti (Esther 1:9, 11–19), among others.

R

RACHAV *(Hebrew)* Large.

RACHEL *(Hebrew)* Purity; little lamb. NOTABLES: Wife of Jacob and the first biblical woman to die in childbirth (Genesis 28:2, 29:6–11, 16–22, 25–31).

Rachel and Her Sister Marry Jacob

Jacob, the son of Isaac and Rebekah, fled the wrath of his brother Esau after he had secured his brother's birthright for himself through deceit. Following his mother's advice, Jacob headed toward the home of his mother's brother, a man named Laban. From Beersheba, Jacob headed for Haran where Laban lived. On the way, night fell. Jacob used rocks for a pillow and the ground for a bed. He dreamed of a ladder stretching from earth to heaven. Angels went up and down the ladder. The Lord appeared above the ladder and told Jacob that he would be given the land on which he slept and that land would become Jacob's and his descendants'. God told Jacob that he would watch over him in all places, wherever he went.

The dream was so powerful that when Jacob awoke, he made an altar out of stones and poured oil upon the top of it (Genesis 28:18). He called the place Beth-el. He made a vow at that altar, stating that if God would be with him, he would one day return to his father's house in peace and the Lord would be his God. Upon the stone pillar he would build God's house.

Jacob continued his journey and eventually arrived in a large field with a stone standing in the center of it. Under the stone was a pool of water, a natural spring. Shepherds had rolled back the stone to allow their sheep to drink. Jacob watched, then approached the shepherds and asked them where they were from. When they told him they were from Haran, Jacob inquired whether or not they knew Laban.

As it turned out, everyone in Haran knew Laban. Jacob inquired about the welfare of his uncle and was told Laban was well. Further, the shepherds pointed out Laban's daughter to Jacob as the woman approached the well with her sheep. Jacob gazed at Rachel as she strolled toward him. Her beauty captivated him. He explained who he was and how he had come to that place and soon discovered that Rachel had a happy and kind temperament. Jacob embraced and kissed his cousin. Rachel ran to her father's house to announce that they would be having a guest staying with them.

Jacob settled in and worked hard for Laban for a month. He refused payment. Laban asked him what he should pay him for his hard work. Jacob had fallen in love and desired Rachel for his wife. He told Laban he would work seven years for his uncle to earn the right marry her. Laban agreed. So Jacob toiled for seven long years, but because it was such a worthy goal, the days passed quickly for him.

Finally his wedding day arrived. Laban began to reconsider his decision to allow the marriage of Jacob to Rachel. His other daughter, Leah, was older than Rachel and remained as yet unmarried. Laban felt it was not right to marry off the younger daughter before the older one was settled. At the wedding festivities, Laban put a dark veil over Leah's face and married her to Jacob. When Jacob opened his eyes the next morning and looked over at his new wife, shock raced through him like a bolt of lightening. Leah, not Rachel, slept beside him.

Infuriated, Jacob dashed out of the tent to seek Laban. He demanded to know why Laban had deceived him. Laban explained that in his country, the older daughter must be married first. Then he told Jacob that he could marry Rachel if he waited one week. The only hitch was that Jacob would now need to work for Laban another seven years.

Jacob had little choice but to agree. That is how he came to have two sisters as wives.

RAHAB *(Hebrew)* Pride. **NOTABLES:** Biblical woman known as the harlot of Jericho. She protected Joshua's men from being discovered by the king of Jericho, who knew that the men had come to spy on Jericho (Joshua 2:1–21).

RAIZEL *(Hebrew)* Rose.

RANITA *(Hebrew)* A joyful song.

RAYNA *(Hebrew/Scandinavian)* Song; counsel.

REBEKAH *(Hebrew)* To tie. **NOTABLES:** Hebrew woman who was wife of Isaac and mother of the Bible's first twins, Esau and Jacob (Genesis 25:25–26). **VARIATIONS:** Becca, Becky, Reba, Rebecca.

RENA *(Greek)* Peace; form of Irene *(Hebrew)* melody.

RENITA *(Latin)* Resistant. **VARIATIONS:** Reneeta, Renyta.

REUMAH *(Hebrew)* Sublime. **NOTABLES:** Concubine of Abraham's brother, Nahor (Genesis 22:23–24).

RHODA *(Greek)* Rose. **NOTABLES:** Christian household servant of John Mark's mother (Acts 12:13–17).

RIMONA *(Hebrew)* Pomegranate.

RINA *(Hebrew)* Joyful song.

RISHONA *(Hebrew)* Primary; first.

RIVKA *(Hebrew)* Noose or knotted cord; to bind or link together.

RIZPAH *(Hebrew)* Coal; hot stone; one who traps.
NOTABLES: Daughter of Aiah and concubine of King
Saul (2 Samuel 3:7, 21:8–11).

Rizpah Showed Strength in Powerlessness

Rizpah was the daughter of the Edomite named Aiah,
one of the tribes that lived in the Negev desert near
Jordan in what is today southern Israel. She was a concubine of King Saul and bore him sons named Armoni
and Mephibosheth.

After Saul fell upon his sword rather than be killed
by the Philistines, the land suffered from famine for
three terrible years. David, who became king after Saul,
prayed to the Lord each year to find out why. He was told
that it was "for Saul, and for his bloody house, because
he slew the Gibeonites" (2 Samuel 21:1). Although Saul
had tried, he had not eradicated the Gibeonites from
the land. The Bible states that they were not the children of Israel but a remnant of the Amorites. David
went to the Gibeonites and sought to redress Saul's
oppression of them. The Gibeonites told him that the
situation required the death of seven of Saul's descendants. David allowed the men to be murdered.

Among the dead, left on the side of a mountain,
were Rizpah's sons and five sons of Merab, the daughter of Saul. The men of Rizpah's family were left lying
uncovered upon the open ground where wild animals
could pick at them. Rizpah went to the site of the murders. She laid sackcloth upon a rock, sat down, and
mourned them day and night for over five months.
The Bible states that "Rizpah the daughter of Aiah

took sackcloth, and spread it for her upon the rock, from the beginning of harvest until water dropped upon them out of heaven, and suffered neither the birds of the air to rest on them by day, nor the beasts of the field by night. And it was told to David what Rizpah the daughter of Aiah, the concubine of Saul, had done" (2 Samuel 21:10–11).

David took pity upon her and had the bodies buried, and not only the bodies of those slain by the Gibeonites in their act of revenge, but also the bodies of Saul and his son Jonathan that had been hung on display by the Philistines and then later stolen by people living in Jabesh-Gilead. David buried the bodies of the house of Saul in the tomb of Kish, who was Saul's father (2 Samuel 21:12–14).

The famine did not end with the murders by the Gibeonites of the male members of Rizpah's family. It was only after David buried them that the famine ended. And the cycle of violence that started during Saul's reign and continued into David's ended with Rizpah's quiet but spiritually profound vigil.

ROMA *(Hebrew)* Lofty; exalted.

RUTH *(Hebrew)* Compassionate friend. NOTABLES: An ancient Moabitess who was daughter-in-law of Naomi and who became the wife of Boaz, Naomi's relative (Book of Ruth, also Matthew 1:5).

Ruth's Bond with Naomi and Boaz

Ruth was a Moabite. Her father had settled in Moab and she had grown up there. When she was of marriageable age, Ruth became the wife of Mahlon, the son of Naomi. Naomi had traveled to Moab with her husband, Elimelech, and two sons during the famine in Judah. Both her boys had married local women. But when Naomi's husband and two boys passed away, she longed to return to Bethlehem. It was too difficult for her and her two daughters-in-laws to find food. Starving, they vowed to leave Moab and return to Bethlehem to Naomi's old house.

They set out upon the road and traveled a short distance before Naomi encouraged the young women to turn back and stay with their own people. Orpah did turn back, but Ruth remained steadfast in her determination to stay with Naomi. She told Naomi, "Intreat me not to leave thee, or to return from following after thee: for whither thou goest, I will go; and where thou lodgest, I will lodge: thy people shall be my people, and thy God my God: Where thou diest, will I die, and there will I be buried: the Lord do so to me, and more also, if ought but death part thee and me" (Ruth 1:16–17).

Naomi's heart was touched by Ruth's words, and the two stayed together. Finally, after the long journey to Bethlehem, they found Naomi's house and settled in. Naomi's friends rushed to welcome her home. She told them to call her *Mara*, a name that meant "bitterness" because with the famine and the death of her husband and two sons, she felt as though God had dealt bitterly with her (Ruth 1:20–21).

The barley harvest had just begun. Naomi told Ruth to go to the field of Boaz to search for some grain. He was a wealthy man who owned a lot of land and could afford to pay workers to harvest his grain.

Boaz noticed her in his field. He asked who she was and was told that she had come to town with Naomi. They both had been in Moab. Boaz didn't mind Ruth picking up leftover grain but worried that one of the workers might bother her. He instructed his men to stay away from her. Then he went to Ruth and told her to work in one of his fields where the women did the harvesting. Ruth felt deep gratitude toward Boaz and thanked him before leaving. But Boaz did not want her to leave just yet. He asked her to stay and have lunch with him. And he even gave her six measures of grain to take back to Naomi.

Naomi and Ruth talked about how Ruth might marry Boaz. Naomi told her to wash and put scented oil upon her body, and then go to his house after dark, slip into his room, and hide while he was eating his evening meal and drinking his wine. When he was resting, she was to uncover his feet and lie down next to him. Ruth followed her mother-in-law's instructions.

Boaz woke at midnight and turned himself only to find Ruth lying next to him. Unsure of who she might be in the dark, he asked, and she answered, "I am Ruth thine handmaid: spread therefore thy skirt over thine handmaid; for thou art a near kinsman" (Ruth 3:8–9). Ruth wanted Boaz to be her guardian.

Boaz agreed to her request. Boaz cleverly overcame any obstacles to marrying Ruth. He was eighty and she was forty years old. Right away, Ruth conceived a son that they named Obed. In time, the child brought laughter to Naomi's lips and lightness to her heart again.

S

SABRA *(Arabic)* Morning.

SADIE *(Hebrew)* Princess; form of Sarah.

SALOME *(Latin)* Peaceful; perfect. NOTABLES: Daughter of Herodias who danced and asked for the head of John the Baptist (Matthew 14:3–12; Mark 6:17–29; Luke 3:19–20). Another biblical Salome was wife of Zebedee and faithful follower of Jesus (Matthew 20:20–23; Mark 15:40–41).

Salome, One of the Women Supporters of Jesus

In most cases, women in biblical times were often identified by the name of the male head of their household. Salome was wife of Zebedee and mother of James and John, who became disciples of Jesus. Jesus called them Boanerges, meaning "sons of thunder" (Mark 3:17).

As for Salome, the Hebrew version of her name may have been spelled Shulamit or Shulamith and the Hellenized form was Salome. Her sons had a fishing business with Simon Peter and Andrew, two other disciples of Jesus. Salome, too, was a faithful follower. The New Testament gospels do not call her a disciple of Jesus but state that she was with his mother Mary, Mary Magdalene, and other women at the cross when Jesus was put to death. Some sources assert that she may have been in some way related to the family of Jesus. The Gospel of Mark states: "There were also women looking on afar off: among whom was Mary

Magdalene, and Mary the mother of James the less and of Joses, and Salome: (who also, when he was in Galilee, followed him, and ministered unto him;) and many other women which came up with him unto Jerusalem" (Mark 15:40–41). Other gospel passages mention Salome, including Matthew 27:56 and Mark 16:1.

After the crucifixion of Jesus, Salome accompanied the other women who went to the tomb to anoint the body. They took with them certain unguents and spices. "And when the Sabbath was past, Mary Magdalene, and Mary the mother of James, and Salome, had bought sweet spices, that they might come and anoint him. And very early in the morning of the first day of the week, they came unto the sepulchre at the rising of the sun" (Mark 16:1–2).

During Jesus' last trip to Jerusalem, Salome had asked him to give her assurances that one of her sons could sit on his right hand and the other on his left in the kingdom of heaven (Matthew 20:21). Her sons also wanted this promise (Mark 10:37). Jesus told them that they could drink from the cup from which he had to drink and be baptized with the suffering he had to endure but he could not grant them their desire to sit at his right and the other at his left for it was not his gift to give (Mark 10:38-40). Salome had raised two boys who became two important people within Jesus' inner circle and she wanted them to be among the elite of Jesus' group in heaven. Jesus told her it was for God to decide.

SAMANTHA *(Hebrew)* Informed by God.

SAMARA *(Hebrew)* Protected by God.

SAMIRA *(Hebrew)* Evening talk.

SAMUELA *(Hebrew)* God hears; feminine form of Samuel.

SAPPHIRA *(Greek)* Beautiful. NOTABLES: Wife of Ananias who convinced her husband to deceive the Apostles about the sale price their property fetched (Acts 5:1–11).

The High Price of Greed: A Story of Sapphira

Ananias and his wife, Sapphira, lived in Jerusalem. They were followers of Jesus during the time of the Apostles, after the death of Jesus. Ananias and Sapphira sold a certain field that they owned. As followers of Christ, they were accustomed to sharing their money for the greater good of the group and for the cost of spreading the Gospel message. The other early Christians were generous in their giving, and their generosity stood in high contrast to the selfish act of Ananias and Sapphira. The couple deceived the church members about the amount of money that they received from the sale of the field in order to keep a portion for themselves.

The Apostle Peter, however, could not be fooled. He confronted Ananias: "why hath Satan filled thine heart to lie to the Holy Ghost, and to keep back part of the price of the land?" (Acts 5:3). It was one thing to hold back the money but quite another to lie to God and his servants. Peter asked Ananias basically how he had become so powerless. After all, he had power over Satan when he owned the land. He had power over Satan after the land was sold. Somehow Satan had taken hold and enabled Ananias to conceive of a plan to cheat and lie. "And Ananias hearing these words fell down, and gave up the ghost: and great fear came on all them that heard these things" (Acts 5:5).

Not long thereafter, some young men came in, bound the body of Ananias, took him away, and buried him. Three hours passed. Sapphira went to find her husband. When she met Peter, he asked her a question. "Tell me whether ye sold the land for so much?" And she said, "Yea, for so much." Then Peter said unto her, How is it that ye have agreed together to tempt the Spirit of the Lord? Behold the feet of them which have buried thy husband are at the door, and shall carry thee out" (Acts 5:8–9). Sapphira, upon hearing his words, dropped at Peter's feet, and died. And she was buried with her husband.

The story of the couple spread throughout the early Christian community and was told and retold to emphasize the power of the Holy Spirit, and also to make the point that Christians must take responsibility for their moral behavior or lack of it.

SARAH *(Hebrew)* Princess. NOTABLES: Wife of Abraham who was barren until she was ninety and then bore a son named Isaac (Genesis 11:29–31); daughter of Asher (Numbers 26:46).

The Annunciation of the Birth of Isaac: A Story of Sarah

The Lord appeared to Abraham in the plains of Mamre while Abraham sat in the doorway of his tent trying to escape the heat of the day. Before him stood three men—actually angels. Abraham rose and went to meet them, bowing low before them. He offered food and water and a place for them to sit and refresh themselves under the tree near his tent. Then he went to find his wife Sarah to prepare some meat. One of them asked Abraham where his wife Sarah was. Abraham told them that she was inside the tent.

The man told Abraham that "lo, Sarah thy wife shall have a son. And Sarah heard it in the tent door, which was behind him" (Genesis 18:10).

Sarah had already gone through a woman's change of life. She laughed in disbelief. The man must have heard her, because he inquired of Abraham why Sarah had laughed. Did she not believe that all things are possible with the Lord? Sarah denied laughing. She said she was afraid. The men rose and left. The truth of their statements was made manifest when Sarah conceived and bore Isaac when she was ninety years old. Sarah died at Hebron when she was one hundred and twenty-seven years old.

SARAI *(Hebrew)* Form of Sarah; original name of Sarah.

SEAMA *(Hebrew)* Treasure. VARIATIONS: Seema, Sima.

SELIMA *(Hebrew)* Peace.

SERACH *(Hebrew)* Plenty.

SHALOM *(Hebrew)* Peace. VARIATIONS: Shalome, Shalva, Shelom, Shilom, Sholome.

SHAMIRA *(Hebrew)* Defender. VARIATIONS: Shameera.

SHANA *(Hebrew)* Beautiful. VARIATIONS: Shan, Shanah, Shandi, Shania, Shayna.

SHARON *(Hebrew)* The fertile plain at the base of Mount Carmel.

SHAVONNE *(Hebrew)* The Lord is gracious. VARIATIONS: Shavon, Shevon, Shivonne, Shyvon, Shyvonne.

SHEBA *(Hebrew)* Promised daughter; short form of Bathsheba.

SHELOMITH *(Hebrew)* My peace; my recompense. NOTABLES: The Israelite woman from the tribe of Dan whose son blasphemed the name of the Lord (Leviticus 24:10–11).

SHERAH *(Hebrew)* Light.

SHIFRA *(Hebrew)* Improved; does well. NOTABLES: The midwife who was the partner of Puah and who saved newborn Jewish boys from death by disobeying Pharaoh's order. (Exodus 1:15–22). VARIATIONS: Shiphrah.

SHILOH *(Hebrew)* Who is to be sent; the peaceful one.

SHIRA *(Hebrew)* Song. VARIATIONS: Shiri.

SHOMER *(Hebrew)* Guard; keep; observe.

SHOSHANA *(Hebrew)* Lily. VARIATIONS: Sosha, Shoshanna.

SIDRA *(Latin)* Stars. VARIATIONS: Cidra, Cydra, Sidri, Sidria, Sydra.

SIMCHA *(Hebrew)* Joyous, festive.

SUE *(Hebrew)* Short form of Susan.

SUSAN *(Hebrew)* Lily. VARIATIONS: Susann, Susanna, Susanne, Susetta, Susette, Susi, Susie, Susy, Suz, Suzane, Suzanna, Suzannah, Suzanne, Suzetta, Suzette, Suzi, Suzie, Zsa Zsa, Zusa, Zuza.

SUSANNA *(Hebrew)* Form of Susan. NOTABLES: Truthful daughter of Hilkiah who was saved from two lusting men who were judges (Susanna 1:1-64); a woman cured of evil spirits and ailments (Luke 8:1–3).

Susanna's Ordeal

Susanna, the lovely and pious daughter of Hilkiah, was married to a wealthy Jew in Babylon. Joakim, her husband, owned a house with a beautiful garden that Susanna enjoyed walking in each day. Joakim had the admiration of many in Babylon. Two judges who came to Joakim's house every day to hold court and hear cases began to admire Susanna. The attraction the two had for Susanna evolved into lust and a desire to have carnal knowledge of her. But they confessed their desire to no one else.

On one particular day at the noon hour, the men left Susanna and Joakim's house to go to their own homes for a meal. But then, without knowing that the other had done the same thing, each judge turned back to Joakim's home. When they saw each other, they both confessed their deep feelings of lust for Joakim's wife. They decided to find the right opportunity to seduce her.

After some time, the men noticed her in the garden. The afternoon heat was stifling. Susanna decided to bathe in the garden, but first told her servants to lock the gate and shut the doors. Neither Susanna nor her maidservants knew that the two judges were already in the garden, hiding among the greenery.

After the maids had brought scented oils and the things Susanna needed, they left. Susanna believed she was alone in the garden. However, the two judges stepped forth and showed themselves to her. They told her of their uncontrollable need to be with her. Susanna was afraid. She knew that to lie with them would ensure her death. But to resist them would mean she would stand trial in their court. She might be sentenced to death.

She screamed and fought off their advances. The maids returned to the garden. Villagers soon joined them. The men denied lying in wait to trap her into making love to them. It was decided that Susanna would have to testify to what had happened.

Crowds packed the house of Joakim. Susanna stood for trial with all her relatives by her side. The men stated their case. They told how she had been there with a young man and had lain with him. The judges tried to save her from the young man's advances, but upon seeing them, he ran away. Though their story was nothing more than a string of lies, the people believed the judges. Susanna was sentenced to death (Daniel 13:41).

She called upon the Lord. She cried out that the judges had lied. As she was being escorted away from her home, the Holy Spirit descended upon Daniel, a man who said he believed her and did not desire to kill her. He chastised those present asking how they could kill her without hearing all the evidence. Daniel made the men go to separate areas where he questioned them without the other present. One man told him that Susanna had lain with her lover under a mastic tree. The other man claimed the tree in question had been an evergreen oak. Neither tree apparently grew in that particular garden, for Daniel had both men put to death that day and preserved Susanna's pristine reputation.

SYNTYCHE *(Hebrew)* That speaks or discourses. NOTABLES: Euodias and Syntyche were female evangelists and associates of the Apostle Paul (Philippians 4:2–3).

T

TABITHA *(Aramaic)* Clear-sighted, gazelle. NOTABLES: A Christian woman named Tabitha (Dorcas in Greek) who lived in Joppa and sewed clothes for widows and was raised from the dead by the Apostle Peter (Acts 9:36–42).

TAHPENES *(Hebrew)* Temptation.

TALIA *(Hebrew)* Morning dew.

TALMA *(Hebrew)* Wiping away; blotting out.

TAMAR *(Hebrew)* Palm; palm tree. NOTABLES: Through an act of lovemaking with her father-in-law, Tamar became the mother of twins, Pharez and Zarah (Genesis 38:24–30). VARIATIONS: Tamara.

Acts of the Children of King David: A Story of Tamar

Tamar was the stepsister of Amnon, heir to the throne of King David, and his brother Absalom. She lived with her mother in quarters separate from the king and from David's various other wives and concubines. Tamar was a beautiful young woman and Amnon longed to know her as a lover. One of his friends urged him to make a conquest of her. The plan was for Amnon to feign some kind of illness and seek solace from Tamar.

The first person to respond to his plea for help because of his sickness was his father, the king. This actually proved fortuitous, for Amnon asked David to ensure that Tamar was sent to bring him food and to feed him.

Beautiful Tamar, wearing the colorful clothes of a king's daughter who was yet a virgin, found herself alone with Amnon in his sleeping room. He looked at her and allowed himself to feel the full extent of his lust. He commanded her to lie with him. Tamar told him not to force her to do such an ungodly thing. She kept her wits and tried every way she knew to dissuade him from forcing himself upon her, but in the end Amnon cared little for the dishonor he would bring upon himself or the shame she would bear. He used his strength to overpower her (2 Samuel 13:14).

Then he despised her more than he loved her. He could no longer stand the sight of her and called his servant to take her away, telling him to "bolt the door after her" (2 Samuel 13:17). Tamar was inconsolable. She put ashes on her head and tore her clothes in a display of utter despair and grief. Weeping, she encountered Absalom. Patient and loving, he pressed her for the truth. Then he took her into the safety of his house and encouraged her not to speak of it. He harbored an intense dislike for his brother from that moment on, yet he did not speak ill of Amnon. King David learned of the unfortunate incident, but did nothing about it. Most likely, this further antagonized Absalom. He vowed to deal with his brother over what he had done to Tamar.

Two years passed. Absalom waited until the timing was right to avenge Tamar. It came one day at the sheep-shearing festival. David usually attended, but that year he sent Amnon as his representative. After Amnon was quite drunk from wine, Absalom's men killed him. Tamar was avenged.

King David was furious. He mourned the loss of his eldest son and banished Absalom from his court. Absalom, however, used his time in exile to rally support for the overthrow of the king. Finally, after time had passed, the king's heart softened toward his exiled son and he invited him home. Absalom attempted to raise a coup; it failed, and he perished.

TAMRA *(Hebrew)* Short form of Tamara.

TEMA *(Hebrew)* Admirable.

THADDINE *(Hebrew)* Exalted; praised.

THERESA *(Greek)* Harvest.

THIRZA *(Hebrew)* Delightful; benevolent; pleasing. VARIATIONS: Tirzah.

THYATIRA *(Hebrew)* Perfume.

TIMNA *(Hebrew)* Forbidding. NOTABLES: Concubine to Eliphaz, son of Esau (Genesis 36:12).

TIVONA *(Hebrew)* Admirer of nature.

TOBY *(Hebrew)* The Lord is good.

TOVE *(Hebrew)* Good. VARIATIONS: Tovah, Tova.

TRYPHENA *(Ancient Greek)* Delicate and tasty. NOTABLES: Member of the early Christian church at Cenchrea that the Apostle Paul salutes in his second letter to the Romans (Romans 16:12). VARIATION: Tryphosa *(Ancient Greek)*.

TZIPPORAH *(Hebrew)* Bird.

U

UDIYA *(Hebrew)* Fire of God.

URIELA *(Hebrew)* Light of the Lord.

URIAIH *(Hebrew)* Light.

URIT *(Hebrew)* Brightness.

USHRIYA *(Hebrew)* The Lord's blessing.

V

VARDA *(Hebrew)* Rose.

VASHTI *(Persian)* Beautiful. NOTABLES: Wife of King Ahasuerus of Persia who offended the king by refusing to go to his banquet after he had sent seven eunuchs to accompany her (Esther 1:9–20).

VERA *(Latin)* True. VARIATIONS: Veera, Veira, Verasha, Viera.

VERITY *(Latin)* Truth. VARIATIONS: Verita, Veriti, Veritie.

VIDETTE *(Hebrew)* The beloved.

VIRTUE *(Latin)* Virtue.

VITA *(Latin)* Life. VARIATIONS: Veeta, Vitel, Vitella.

W

WINIFRED *(Welsh)* Holy peace. VARIATIONS: Win, Winifrede, Winifride, Winifryde, Winne, Winni, Winnie, Winny, Wyn, Wynn.

WISDOM *(English)* Wisdom.

Y

YADIRA *(Hebrew)* Friend.

YAEL *(Hebrew)* To ascend; form of Jael.

YAFFA *(Hebrew)* Beautiful.

YARDENA *(Hebrew)* To descend.

YARKONA *(Hebrew)* Green.

YEHUDIT *(Hebrew)* Praise; form of Judith.

YEMINA *(Hebrew)* Strong. VARIATIONS: Yemena.

YENTA *(Hebrew)* Tattle-tale; gossip.

YENTL *(Hebrew)* Kind.

YESHARA *(Hebrew)* Pointed.

YOANA *(Hebrew)* The Lord is gracious; form of Joanna. VARIATIONS: Yoanna, Yona.

YONINA *(Hebrew)* Dove.

YORDAN *(Hebrew)* Descend; form of Jordan.

YOYELA *(Hebrew)* Rejoicing.

Z

ZACHARI *(Hebrew)* God remembers.

ZAHAVA *(Hebrew)* Golden.

ZAKIAH *(Hebrew)* Pure. VARIATIONS: Zaka, Zakah, Zaki, Zakia, Zakiah, Zakiya, Zakiyya.

ZARA *(Hebrew)* Dawn. VARIATIONS: Zahra, Zaria.

ZAYIT *(Hebrew)* Olive.

ZEFIRA *(Hebrew)* Morning.

ZEHARA *(Hebrew)* Light.

ZEHAVA *(Hebrew)* Gold.

ZEHIRA *(Hebrew)* Careful.

ZEMIRA *(Hebrew)* Song of joy; vine.

ZEMORAH *(Hebrew)* Tree branch.

ZENANA *(Hebrew)* Woman. VARIATIONS: Zena, Zenia.

ZENDA *(Hebrew)* Holy.

ZERA *(Hebrew)* Seeds.

ZERESH *(Hebrew)* Misery; scattered inheritance.

ZERLINDA *(Hebrew)* Beautiful dawn. VARIATIONS: Zerlina.

ZERUIAH *(Hebrew)* Wasp; hornet. NOTABLES: Daughter of Jesse, sister of Abigail (1 Chronicles 2:16).

ZERUIAH *(Hebrew)* Balsam. NOTABLES: David's sister who produced several sons mentioned in the Bible as great warriors (1 Chronicles 2:15–16; 2 Samuel 2:13, 18).

ZETTA *(Hebrew)* Olive.

ZEVIDA *(Hebrew)* Gift.

ZIBIAH *(Hebrew)* The Lord dwells. NOTABLES: Woman from Beer-sheba who became wife of King Ahaziah of Judah and mother of Jehoash (2 Kings 12:1; 2 Chronicles 24:1).

ZILLAH *(Hebrew)* Shadow. NOTABLES: One of two wives taken by Lamech, the first polygamy occurrence in the Bible against God's commandment to take one wife (Genesis 4:19).

ZILPAH *(Hebrew)* Dignity. NOTABLES: Leah's hand-maiden who bore two sons to Leah's husband Jacob (Genesis 46:18).

ZIMRIAH *(Hebrew)* Songs.

ZIPPORAH *(Hebrew)* Bird. NOTABLES: The Midianite wife of Moses who was the first biblical woman to perform a circumcision (Exodus 2:16–22).

Zipporah's Quick Thinking Saves Moses

Zipporah was the daughter of a Midian priest. Her father gave her to Moses as a wife after Moses stopped some shepherds from harassing the young woman and her six sisters at a desert well when they attempted to water their sheep. Moses had fled Egypt, where he had taken the life of a slave owner who had been mistreating a Hebrew. As he sat at the well, he saw the sisters approaching with their animals. When the other shepherds tried to divert the young women from the well, Moses came to their aid and even helped them water their sheep.

Jethro, Zipporah's father, thanked Moses. He gave him a job as a shepherd and also gave him Zipporah as a wife. Although Zipporah was a Midianite and Moses was a Hebrew, the couple forged a good marriage. In time, she and Moses produced two boys, Gershom and Eliezar. The boys were still young when Moses was instructed by God to return to Egypt. There, he was to lead God's chosen ones, the Hebrews, from bondage to freedom in the Promised Land.

A strange event occurred as the family traveled back to Egypt. They stopped to rest at an inn. While there, the Lord sought to kill Moses (Exodus 4:24). Zipporah, perhaps believing that they had offended God by not circumcising their sons, grabbed a sharp stone and circumcised one of her boys (the Bible does not reveal which one). Then holding the bloody fore-skin before Moses (perhaps in front of his genitalia, for the Bible says she "cast it at his feet" and feet is a biblical euphemism for genitals), she said "Surely a bloody husband art thou to me" (Exodus 4:25). The Bible does not say whether or not Moses, who was raised in Egypt, was ever circumcised. God must have been satisfied with the child serving as the substitute for he let Moses go. Zipporah reiterated her words. Thanks to her quick thinking, her husband's life was spared and he was able to continue the work God had commanded him to do—that is, lead the children of God out of Egyptian bondage.

ZIRAH *(Hebrew)* Coliseum.

ZITA *(Hebrew)* Seeker.

ZIZ *(Hebrew)* Flower; cleft; wadi; pass. NOTABLES: A pass or wadi such as the *Ain Jidy*, connecting the shoreline of the Dead Sea into Judah toward Jerusalem through which the Mehunim, Ammonite, and Moabite people had to traverse (2 Chronicles 20:16).

ZOHARA *(Hebrew)* Bright; brilliance.

ZULEMA *(Hebrew)* Peace.

ZURIEL *(Hebrew)* Rock or strength of God.

Resources

Saint Joseph Edition of the New American Bible
Translated from the original languages with critical use of all the ancient sources, including the revised New Testament and the revised Psalms.
New York: Catholic Book Publishing Co., 1991.

The Holy Bible: Old and New Testaments
Self-pronouncing edition, conforming to the 1611 edition, commonly known as the Authorized or King James Version.
Cleveland and New York: The World Publishing Company. (No copyright or publication date available.)

The New Testament of Our Lord and Saviour Jesus Christ
Translated from the original Greek, Dutch-English edition.
New York: American Bible Society, 1869.

The Books of the Old Testament

Genesis	Ecclesiastes
Exodus	The Song of Solomon
Leviticus	Isaiah
Numbers	Jeremiah
Deuteronomy	Lamentations
Joshua	Ezekiel
Judges	Daniel
Ruth	Hosea
1 Samuel	Joel
2 Samuel	Amos
1 Kings	Obadiah
2 Kings	Jonah
1 Chronicles	Micah
2 Chronicles	Nahum
Ezra	Habakkuk
Nehemiah	Zephaniah
Esther	Haggai
Job	Zechariah
Psalms	Malachi
Proverbs	

The Books of the New Testament

Matthew	1 Timothy
Mark	2 Timothy
Luke	Titus
John	Philemon
The Acts	Hebrews
Romans	James
1 Corinthians	1 Peter
2 Corinthians	2 Peter
Galatians	1 John
Ephesians	2 John
Philippians	3 John
Colossians	Jude
1 Thessalonians	Revelation
2 Thessalonians	

Index